# Living Above
## YOUR
# Circumstances

## BOB GEORGE

**HARVEST HOUSE PUBLISHERS**
Eugene, Oregon 97402

Unless otherwise indicated, all Scripture quotations are taken from the Holy Bible, New International Version ®. Copyright © 1973, 1978, 1984 by the International Bible Society. Used by permission of Zondervan Publishing House. The "NIV" and "New International Version" trademarks are registered in the United States Patent and Trademark Office by International Bible Society.

Verses marked KJV are taken from the King James Version of the Bible.

Verses marked NASB are taken from the New American Standard Bible, © 1960, 1962, 1963, 1968, 1971, 1972, 1973, 1975, 1977 by The Lockman Foundation. Used by permission.

Cover by Terry Dugan Design, Minneapolis, Minnesota.

## LIVING ABOVE YOUR CIRCUMSTANCES

Copyright © 1996 by Harvest House Publishers
Eugene, Oregon 97402

Library of Congress Cataloging-in-Publication Data

George, Bob, 1933–
    Living above your circumstances / Bob George.
        p.   cm.
    ISBN 1-56507-415-7 (alk. paper)
    1. Christian life.   I. Title.
  BV4501.2G425   1996
  248.4—dc20
                                                  96-26320
                                                    CIP

**All rights reserved.** No portion of this book may be reproduced in any form without the written permission of the Publisher.

**Printed in the United States of America.**

96   97   98   99   00   01   /   BF   /   10   9   8   7   6   5   4   3   2   1

# Contents

## *Special Thanks*

I want to express my love and special thanks to my wife Amy for her dedication to the Lord and her unending faithfulness to me. She has lived through all of the experiences mentioned in this book and could have just as well been the author.

I also want to give a special thanks to Al Janssen, who helped to organize and put my thoughts into manuscript form. To Bob Christopher and the other members of the *People to People* staff, who contributed to the completion of this book, I say, "Thanks—you all are the greatest."

# Introduction

It's difficult for me to believe that by the time this book is published, I will have been in Christ for well over 27 years. In that length of time, I have had the marvelous experience of counseling literally thousands of people through both live radio and personal interaction. I have also had the privilege of traveling to many areas of the world and meeting people from all walks of life, from every economic strata, and of all colors and creeds. Even with all this diversity, I have found that every human heart shares a common thread of truth: *Fear is man's greatest enemy, and love is man's greatest friend*.

No matter where you go in the world, everyone responds in the same way to negative circumstances. And Satan influences us all in the same way. When we are going through difficult times he keeps us living in a continual state of fear by convincing us that we alone are the only resource available to change our circumstances and to solve all our problems. Deep down in our hearts we know that this is an exercise in futility; it is like trying to hold ten corks under water at the same time. Yet, in quiet desperation, we keep on trying to change and to control our circumstances in fear of being totally crushed by them. Most of our lives are spent trying to climb out from under our circumstances instead of turning to the One who alone can teach us how to live above them.

Through the years I have learned that all of us experience hardships in one form or another. We have all been insulted, injured, or rejected by others. We all have problems—with our marriage, friends, children, job, finances, or destructive habits. And problems are a fact of life! Jesus told us that in this world we are going to have tribulation.

But we do not have to be afraid, because He has overcome the world.

I'm sure that you are familiar with the fear that accompanies adverse circumstances. Fear is a natural response to life's problems. When we experience the emotion of fear, we usually want to get rid of it. However, the issue isn't how to eliminate fear, but what to do with it. The Bible tells us to cast all our anxieties on Him because He cares for us (1 Peter 5:7). Why is this important? Quite simply, if we do not transfer them to Christ, we will be forced to try to control whomever or whatever is causing the fear in our life. When we attempt to take control, we end up shifting the responsibility for our happiness onto ourselves rather than on our Creator. In doing so, we dedicate ourselves to a life of self-effort that will always result in strife and stress. I have found in life that if I have to strive to get something, then I will also have to strive to keep what I get.

In the book of Philippians we are told, "Do not be anxious about anything, but in everything, by prayer and petition, with thanksgiving, present your requests to God. And the *peace of God*, which transcends all understanding, will guard your hearts and your minds in Christ Jesus" (4:6-7, emphasis added).

The world's search for peace is universal in scope. Man's desire to achieve peace, and his failure to do so, is the main subject of every newspaper in the world. I have come to realize that you can never have international peace until you have national peace. You cannot have national peace until you have local peace. You cannot have local peace until you have peace within your own home. And, you cannot have peace within your own home until you have peace within your own heart. This is where the Lord Jesus Christ is relevant to our personal peace as well as to international peace. He is the only One who can replace fear with love, for "there is no fear in love. But perfect love drives out fear" (1 John 4:18). It is only when we learn to transfer our fears and anxieties to the Prince of Peace and the God of love that we will be able to experience the peace of God that passes all understanding (Philippians 4:7).

Jesus said, "I came that they might have life, and might have it abundantly" (John 10:10 NASB). The life that He came to give you is His own. Christ Himself is the Christian life. Only He can give it, and only He can live it. It is His life that will enable you to live above the circumstances in your life. That is what this book is about.

The stories are about real people who have come to know the love of God and, as a result, have been set free from the bondage of fear. It is my prayer that the content of *Living Above Your Circumstances* will help to enrich your life as the truths of Scripture teach you the total sufficiency of our Lord Jesus Christ for every problem you encounter in your life. Indeed, we have been given "everything we need for life and godliness through our knowledge of Him" (2 Peter 1:3). As we learn to shift our dependency upon Him and off of ourselves, we are able to draw upon those resources that are available to each and every one of us.

# 1
## *You are Not Unusual*

John was feeling down and thought he had the flu, so he made an appointment to see his doctor. Little did he expect the alarming news his doctor would give him after he was examined. Blood tests revealed John was HIV positive—he was dying of AIDS as a result of a blood transfusion he received several years earlier.

John was devastated. He had just married the love of his life when he was given this news. Questions raced through his mind: *Why me? What am I being punished for? How did this happen?* With each question, his feelings of fear and anger intensified. He was fearful of what the disease would do to his body. He was angry at the hospital and angry at God for allowing this to happen.

In a totally different situation, a man named Bill was greeted at his office with a pink slip. His company was downsizing, and he did not survive the cut. Bill couldn't help but think about the future: *What will I do? How will I provide for my family?* Bill had never been an anxious person, but on that day anxiety, worry, and fear gripped his heart.

Neither John nor Bill were expecting the adverse circumstance that they encountered; life merely brought them their way. The same can happen to us as well; that is the reality of life for all of us. Jesus said, "In this world you will have trouble" (John 16:33). Notice that He did not say that trouble is something that you may or may not have. He was very clear: Because you live in this world, you *will* have trouble. It is not *if*, but *when*.

If you were ever in doubt about the truthfulness of God's Word, John 16:33 should put those doubts to rest. I have yet to meet anyone who has never encountered trouble.

People lose their jobs, couples divorce, loved ones die, children rebel, friends betray each other, and relationships crumble. The list goes on and on. These circumstances are not unusual. They are part of the human experience...and so are the emotional responses we have to them.

When trouble comes our way, emotions like fear, anger, remorse, disappointment, anxiety, sadness, discouragement, jealousy, and worry are not unusual. They are part of our human experience. If emotional responses were unusual, the Bible would not be filled with statements like, "Be anxious for nothing," "Cast all your cares on Jesus," "Fear not," "In your anger do not sin," and "Do not worry about tomorrow."

Why does God say these things? Is He trying to chastise us or to make us feel guilty when we experience emotions? No; the reason He says, "Be anxious for nothing" is because *He* is the solution to anxiety. He tells us to "fear not" because He is the answer to fear.

So often when we experience problems and the emotional responses that accompany them we think we are the only one who has ever felt the way we do. We conclude that we must be "different." Or, we say, "What's wrong with me?" Or, "How can a Christian respond like this?"

Wally, a member of our ministry staff, recently moved to a new neighborhood. He related to me how his daughter, Erin, came home everyday from school crying. He and his wife, Pam, tried for several weeks to find out what was wrong. Finally, Erin confided that she did not feel like she knew as much as the other kids in her class. She felt lost, embarrassed, and frustrated.

It's not unusual for a person to feel insecure in a new situation or feel awkward when attempting something new. At one time or another we have all felt this way. Erin thought she was the only one in her classroom struggling. To her, it appeared like algebra was second nature to all the other kids.

Erin's emotional responses immediately manifested themselves in her situation. However, that's not how it happens for everyone. For some people, it may take awhile before the full impact of an adverse circumstance is felt.

Let's take a look at the story of James and Ruth, a delightful couple who had been involved with *People to People* for a number of years. One day when they answered the phone they were shocked to hear the voice of a policeman. The officer told them that their son Jamie had been in an accident and was in the intensive care unit of the local hospital.

This accident happened shortly before Jamie was to graduate from high school. His future looked bright and very promising; he had just received an academic scholarship to a major university. His life seemed to be headed for success. Unfortunately, Jamie never recovered consciousness. After several days in the hospital, he died.

In the days that followed, James and Ruth grieved deeply, yet they clung to the truths of God's love and grace. They also relied on the strength and support that came from family and friends. Christ walked them through the most difficult time in their lives, and they experienced His comfort and peace.

Three years later, James began to struggle with questions he felt he should have asked shortly after Jamie's death. Questions like, *Why Jamie? Why us? What if . . . ?* were nagging away at him in the back of his mind. When I talked with him, he said he felt bad because he was asking these questions a long time after Jamie had died. He thought that if he was truly walking by faith, he would not be experiencing this emotional pain now.

He said he didn't want to attend church because to him it seemed that everyone there had their lives together and his was a mess. He didn't feel accepted. How sad that most Christians deny the fact that we are human beings and, as such, possess all of the weaknesses of our humanity!

James' grief is not unusual. We shouldn't think something is wrong with us when we feel pain, shed tears, or experience sorrow—even when those emotional responses come three years after the fact. These are normal human responses to adversity.

Sooner or later, trouble visits everyone. Sometimes the trouble is of our own making. Other times it is caused by the work or decisions of others. Either way, the trials and tribulations of life bring emotional pain. That is not unusual.

## A Key Truth

I have often been asked, "But why do some people seem to rise above their circumstances while others struggle and are barely able to cope?"

Perhaps we can gain some insight into this by looking at the life of the apostle Paul. Paul was a man who lived through some of the most difficult circumstances anyone could ever imagine. In 2 Corinthians 11, he describes what his life was like:

I have...been in prison more frequently, been flogged more severely, and been exposed to death again and again. Five times I received from the Jews the forty lashes minus one. Three times I was beaten with rods, once I was stoned, three times I was shipwrecked, I spent a night and a day in the open sea, I have been constantly on the move. I have been in danger from rivers, in danger from bandits, in danger from my own countrymen, in danger from Gentiles; in danger in the city, in danger in the country, in danger at sea; and in danger from false brothers. I have labored and toiled and have often gone without sleep; I have known hunger and thirst and have often gone without food; I have been cold and naked (verses 23-27).

If that were my life, I would be asking God to get me out of those trials and tribulations. However, God has a higher purpose for us than merely taking away our problems. He wants to teach us about the sufficiency of His love and grace in the midst of our difficulties. Therefore, God's answer for Paul was, "My grace is sufficient for you, for my power is made perfect in weakness" (2 Corinthians 12:9).

---

*God has a higher purpose
for us than merely
taking away our problems.*

---

Paul learned through suffering the secret of how to discover God's power—by first learning to recognize the weakness of his own flesh. He didn't try to hide his weakness or pretend to be somebody he was not. This truth made Paul's heart rejoice and enabled him to say, "I will boast all the more gladly about my weaknesses, so that Christ's power may rest on me. That is why, for Christ's sake, I delight in weaknesses, in insults, in hardships, in persecutions, in difficulties. For when I am weak, then I am strong" (2 Corinthians 12:10).

Those verses used to puzzle me. I could never fully understand their meaning. When I read Paul's words, I would wonder, "How could anyone in their right mind delight in insults, hardships, persecutions, and difficulties?"

Then one day the answer dawned on me. The only way I could ever delight in those things was if God used them to show me the truth about myself: I am weak. My human nature tells me I should be strong, but my normal responses to adverse circumstances prove otherwise. God wants us to recognize our weaknesses and to rejoice in them so that we can turn to the One who is strong.

Most of us have never endured the extreme troubles faced by Paul. Yet, regardless of whether our trials and tribulations are minor or severe, they show that we are not the towers of strength that we think we are. In our humanity, all of us are weak. That is why we usually respond negatively to our problems and become despondent, discouraged, and downhearted. We lose hope when we can't control life, people, or circumstances.

Of course, no one wants to admit openly that he is weak. It is not impressive. Yet Paul rejoiced in his weakness. He wasn't afraid to admit the truth about his human frailties. He delighted in his weakness because it forced him to turn to Christ completely.

The same is true with us. We are not going to eliminate our problems. Neither are we going to change the natural emotions we experience as a result of those problems. We are going to have to come to the truth that in and of ourselves, we are totally incapable of being strong on our own. We have no alternative other than to turn to the One who has overcome the world.

Earlier, I quoted Jesus' words: "In this world, you will have trouble" (John 16:33). We are not strong enough or wise enough to keep trouble away. But Jesus went on to say, "Take heart! I have overcome the world." We cannot overcome the world, but we can live in dependency on the One who already has—Jesus Christ.

## Finding the Right Answer

You may be reading this book in the hope that you'll find answers to problems that are weighing you down. The good news is that God knows your situation and is ready to teach you to trust Him so you can live above your circumstances.

---

*We cannot overcome the world,
but we can live in dependency on the
One who already has—Jesus Christ.*

---

Your problems may not be like those of John, Bill, James and Ruth, or Erin. But perhaps you can identify with elements of their situations. Maybe you live in anger because life seems unfair. Or you are worrying about not having enough income to pay your bills, or wondering how you will save for your children's future and college education. Perhaps you know the fear of losing a loved one or the insecurity of an uncertain future.

Fear and worry are normal, but the world wants you to think that you are unusual when you experience those emotions. Billions of marketing dollars are spent trying to convince you that you have problems that are unusual and that you need to buy their solutions. The world tells you it is unusual to have body odor in order to sell you deodorant. It tells you it is unusual for ordinary men not to have gorgeous women following them around and that's why you need their brand of shampoo, beer, or fancy cars. This thinking can permeate our perspective on circumstances. If you buy into this thinking, you will never find the permanent answers that are available to us in Jesus Christ.

Be leery of the world's answers. Its desire is to lure you into a trap. To a fish, a lure looks like something desirable to eat—if it didn't look desirable, the fish would never bite into it. But when the fish is deceived and bites into the lure, it winds up in a frying pan. We want to make sure we aren't deceived as well.

Just as we must be wary of worldly marketing efforts, we must avoid being deceived by religious thinking and psychological fads that say it is unusual to be fearful, depressed, or anxious. There is nothing unusual about these emotions. They are simply natural responses to adverse circumstances.

Perhaps you know how difficult it is to make a two-year-old child sit still in a church service. We get upset because the child acts naturally. Is it unusual for a kid to be fidgety? Not at all. Two-year-olds are naturally fidgety. Likewise, there is nothing unusual about negative reactions to negative circumstances. There's nothing wrong with you; you don't have to run for help. What you need is a new way of thinking—*a renewed mind*—so you can live above your circumstances.

What I'm going to share with you in this book is not only what I have learned out of the Word of God but have experienced in real life. My wife, Amy and I know what it is like to endure painful rejection from people whom we love. You see, it is oftentimes, the people you care about who can really hurt you. They are the only ones you let close enough to you so that you become vulnerable to their responses. What others might say or think doesn't seem to matter as much. We have experienced deep disappointment leading to depression, and I have been forced to confront the relevancy of my own teaching. Either the truths of Scripture were and are applicable to our circumstances, or they are of no value to anyone.

Every lesson in this book has been pounded out on the anvil of experience, and I can assure you that God's truth *does* set you free. The message I have for you is that His truth works. The pain from rejection hurts, and there is not always instant relief. But, I can assure you that if you diligently apply the insights and teachings of this book you will walk through your circumstances without being crushed by them.

In this book, I want to introduce you to the only One who can take you through any adversity—Jesus Christ. You don't have to feel embarrassed or fearful about going to Him with a problem. It doesn't matter whether your difficulty is big or small. In fact, can you imagine God, who created this universe, would ever think you had a "big" problem? Nothing surprises Him. He is the One who said to cast "all your cares upon Him, for He cares for you" (NKJV). Every man-made solution for finding peace in the midst of the storms of life is temporary at best. Always remember, peace is not the absence of trouble. Rather, it is the presence of God in the midst of trouble. His solution is permanent. I hope you won't settle for anything less than what He provides.

Because emotions are a very real aspect of our response to life's problems, we'll begin by taking a look at how our emotions operate. That's the subject of our next chapter.

# 2

## *Feelings Follow Thought*

Have you ever been angry? Have you ever been jealous or depressed? Certainly all of us can relate to these powerful emotions. Can you remember the thoughts you were thinking at the time when you experienced them? I bet you weren't thinking thoughts of love and tenderness!

Emotions are real but they are *not* unusual. In fact, they are very predictable because emotions respond to what we are thinking. God designed them as responders, not initiators. They instantly and naturally follow whatever we have been thinking about.

Most people don't know what to do with their negative emotions. If you have ever felt a negative emotion, you can understand why so many flock to counselors or therapists to rid themselves of these troublesome feelings. None of us like to feel bad, so we search for instant relief or take something to make us feel better. We think, *If I can just end the emotional pain, everything will be okay.* That sounds good, but life doesn't work that way.

If we want to change our emotions, we must change our thinking.

This truth was amplified in my own life recently when I was driving from Orange County, California, through Los

Angeles to North Hollywood. As I was traveling on the freeway, I noticed a little red light flash on the dashboard of my rental car. The light indicated that it was time to check the engine. It didn't stay on long, so I didn't worry about it. A few minutes later, another car pulled up beside me and the driver frantically gestured that there was something wrong with my car. I rolled down the window and was overwhelmed by the smell of gasoline. I glanced at the gas gauge and it showed that the tank was already half empty, even though I had only driven about 20 miles.

My first thought was, *Where am I going to find a gas station on the Los Angeles freeway? I'll never get to my appointment on time.* Then my imagination kicked in. Before long, I pictured someone driving along beside me, rolling down his window and, as he smiled, flipping a lit cigarette out of his window into the gasoline that was leaking out of my car. Suddenly there was an explosion and my car burst into flames. I desperately tried to release my seat belt, but it wouldn't unlatch. Before long, my clothes were scorched and my body was burned from head to toe. I have always said that the greatest reward I could ever receive from the Lord would be hearing Him say, "Well done, good and faithful servant." Under this circumstance, the words "well done" would have taken on a brand new meaning!

Did my thoughts stop there? No way. I started wondering if my life insurance was paid for and how Amy was going to accept the news that I had been burned up in a car fire in Los Angeles. Before I knew it, I had visualized myself in a casket with all of my friends and relatives streaming by, looking in, and affectionately saying, "Under the circumstances, he looks good."

While this fantasy was playing in my mind, I was anxiously looking for an exit off the freeway and praying that if I lived to get to a gas station, the people there would be able to repair this car. You can imagine my joy when I saw an exit sign. I pulled off the freeway and made my way to a gas station. The attendant told me they didn't have the facilities to repair the car; I would have to drive to another station a mile away. You don't know how happy I was when I arrived at that station and they said they could fix the problem!

While I was driving on the freeway, my thoughts were filled with fear. But now a new set of thoughts came into my mind—thoughts of anger. I became angry about the rental car company's negligence. *They should have known that the gas tank was going to leak!* My anxiety intensified as I realized that I was going to be extremely late for my appointment. Then I began to re-think what might have happened to me had someone truly thrown a cigarette at the gas leaking from my car.

What I was imagining could have happened, but the reality was that it didn't. I *did* make it to a gas station. The car *was* repaired. The rental agency *was* understanding and courteous. And, as it turned out, the people I had an appointment with were also late. We all arrived at approximately the same time.

I wish I could say that I responded with total faith when all this occurred, trusting the Lord to meet my needs. Unfortunately, that is not what happened; instead, I responded with fear, anxiety, and anger. Were these responses unusual? No. They only showed our human tendency to fantasize and think the worse.

## The Power of Emotions

Our emotions have no intellect. They do not analyze whether or not the scene in our mind reflects something that is actually happening or if it is something we conjured up in our imagination. Our emotions simply respond. They cannot discern between fact or fantasy; truth or falsehood; or past, present, and future. Our emotions predictably respond to whatever we are thinking.

And whatever we are feeling, we can only feel it in the now. We cannot feel something yesterday, which is in the past. We can't feel something tomorrow, which is not here yet. The only time we can feel something is *right now.*

You may be dwelling on something that happened yesterday or long ago. You may be thinking about what might happen tomorrow. Or, you may be imagining something that may or may not happen. No matter what the case, your emotions cannot discern the difference. They simply respond as if what you were thinking is happening now.

Let me share with you what happened to a friend of mine, Ann, whom I hadn't seen for nearly 40 years. Her experience is a perfect example of emotions responding to what a person is thinking.

It was 5:30 in the morning when the telephone jarred me out of my sleep at the hotel where I was staying in my hometown of New Castle, Indiana. At first I thought it was a wake-up call. But the woman on the other end said she was calling because she had seen an article in the local newspaper which had reported on my life, my national radio program *People to People,* and my counseling services.

I hadn't seen Ann since I graduated from high school. She graduated one year behind my class, but I knew her quite well because all through school she dated my best friend, Ed. Upon graduation, Ed headed off to college but not before he asked Ann to marry him. Ann wanted to say yes, but felt she couldn't until she had at least finished high school.

"I made a terrible mistake," Ann cried into the telephone. Her story emerged slowly. Ed had started dating someone else in college and ended up marrying that girl instead of Ann. For 40 years, Ann had lived in remorse, guilt, and depression over the imagined perception that she had lost the love of her life and her "only" opportunity for happiness.

"If I had just married Ed, my life would have been so different, so much happier," she sobbed.

By now, Ann was crying uncontrollably over the telephone. "I've been an emotional wreck for the past 40 years. My emotions have been out of control. It seems I fly off the handle when anyone just looks at me. And, my anger boils over when another man looks at me. It seems that I am angry at everyone all the time."

I asked her, "Ann, did it ever enter your mind that the reason that you are feeling angry and sad is because for 40 years you have been thinking angry and sad thoughts?"

Ann answered me as if she thought I was crazy. "Bob, you don't understand. My emotions have been a mess for 40 years."

"I realize that, Ann," I said. "But I'm telling you that you do not have an emotional problem."

She was speechless; now she really seemed confused.

"You see, Ann, your emotions are perfectly healthy," I continued. "They are responding predictably to what you are thinking, just as God designed them to. So, you do not have an emotional problem. You have a thinking problem."

As I probed, I learned that Ann, torn by regret over her decision, had never married and had been in and out of mental hospitals for the past 20 years.

"My doctor has me on tranquilizers so I can sleep. They seem to help my emotions."

"Ann, tranquilizers can numb your mind, which might help your emotions temporarily, but when you wake up and the pills wear off, what happens then?"

"I'm angry and sad all over again," she said.

"That's right," I agreed. "That's because your emotions respond to what's in your mind. And until you change your thinking, you can't expect your emotions to change."

"But you don't understand..."

"Oh, I understand quite well, Ann," I interrupted. "I realize that you have been deeply hurt in the past, and I'm sorry for that, but you are presently living in a fantasy. You believe that if you had married Ed, you would have had a much happier life. But that's a fantasy. I'm sure that if you were to interview Ed's wife, you would find that she hasn't had a perfect life of wine and roses. Ed married another woman. Every time you think about that, you get angry. As long as you continue to think those same angry and sad thoughts, you will continue to feel angry and sad. So, if you want to change how you *feel*, you have to change your *thinking*.

"Don't you see, Ann, that you have convinced yourself that if you had married your high school sweetheart, everything would have turned out romantically wonderful? That thought has caused you to live entrapped in your own misery for 40-plus years. My question to you, Ann, is this: Do you want to get well?"

---

*If you want to change how you feel, you have to change your thinking.*

---

After a brief pause, Ann tearfully admitted that she wanted relief from her misery. That was a very important first step. I then walked her through the steps that will be outlined in the next few chapters. After about an hour on the telephone, I could sense the relief in Ann's voice as though a heavy weight had been lifted off her shoulders. She finally understood the relationship between her thinking and her emotions and realized that there had to be a change in her thinking in order to get well.

I sent Ann a tape series I did a few years ago, entitled *How to Experience Victory Over Depression*. A couple of months later, I received a letter from her stating how the contents of those tapes were changing her life.

About a year later, some friends of mine in Indianapolis had an open house for me, and we invited a number of people from my hometown. Many of my old friends attended, including Ed, his wife, and Ann. During the evening, I asked Ann how she was doing. She said, "I'm doing much better. I've slipped a couple of times into my old thinking patterns and found myself starting to explode all over again. Then I realized what was going on in my thoughts and, within minutes, brought myself back to reality and my emotions stabilized."

I asked her how she felt being at a gathering with Ed present. She answered, "There's still a tinge of pain that remains, but I am 100 percent better."

## The Need to Make a Choice

I believe the key question I asked Ann was, "Do you want to get well?" Notice that I didn't ask, "Do you want to change your circumstances?" That is not the issue. In many cases you can't change your circumstances, but you can decide how you will respond to them. You don't have to get angry. You don't have to plunge into depression. You do have a choice. You can continue to hold on to old attitudes, premises, hard feelings, or thinking habits that produce depression. Or, you can choose to allow God to transform your mind. This approach produces peace.

All of us need to learn to face life in all of its reality and think soberly in regard to the circumstances that come our way (Romans 12:3). Remember, Jesus said, "In this world you will have trouble" (John 16:33).

Realizing we will have difficult circumstances come our way can help cushion their impact. But knowing that

Christ is the only stabilizer during our storms can equip us to face life head on.

Not too long ago, my secretary, Jodi, and her husband, Joe, experienced an adverse circumstance that helped them realize their weakness and the importance of trusting in Christ. For over ten years, they had tried desperately to start a family. They faithfully followed every suggestion from their doctor, but nothing brought about a pregnancy.

---

> *You might not be able to*
> *change your circumstances,*
> *but you can decide how you will*
> *respond to them.*

---

One day, Jodi burst into the office with a big smile on her face and with an excitement that could have meant only one thing—she was pregnant! Everyone in the office, their family, and their friends rejoiced at the good news. Jodi and Joe's dream of bringing a child into the world was finally coming true. Joe could already see himself teaching "little Joe" how to fish, swim, and ride a bicycle.

Two months later, their joy turned to sorrow. Jodi suffered a miscarriage...and a cloud of sadness shrouded everyone.

It is in times like this, in the crunches of life, that we have a decision to make. Jodi and Joe knew they could either spend the next few months, and possibly years, grieving and hurting over the loss of their baby, or they could decide to rejoice in what they had. They had each other. They had good health. They had Christ as their Savior, and a living hope that they would have another chance to have a baby. They could choose to experience the peace of God that passes all understanding—even in the midst of their disappointment.

Because Jodi and Joe trusted Christ, they experienced His peace and joy. At the point of their need, He loved them through their pain. His love, joy, and peace came from their dependency upon Him during the most difficult moment of their lives.

When troubles come our way, it isn't unusual for us to experience certain emotions, although the world would have us thinking otherwise. In and of themselves, emotions are neither bad nor good. As I have said, they are merely responders to whatever we are putting into our minds. And this is exactly how God designed them to work.

Remember the stories about John and Bill in chapter 1? John was feeling devastated after he heard the news that he was HIV positive. His situation forced him to experience worry and fear: *What is going to happen now? How much longer do I have to live? What will happen to my wife? Am I being punished for not living as good a life as I should have? Why wasn't the hospital more careful?*

John's mind was racing from the present to the past to the future and back. The only emotions such thoughts can produce are fear and anger. They were predictable responses to what he was thinking.

Bill had received a pink slip from his employer. Could he have felt anything other than anxiety when he wondered what he would do next and how he could provide for his family? His thoughts focused on the uncertainties of the future, and anxiety was the natural emotional response.

By now I'm sure you can see that it is not our emotions that need to be corrected. Our emotions, whether we are feeling anxious or happy, are working just fine and exactly as God designed them. It is our *thinking* that needs to be renewed if we are going to learn to live above our circumstances.

# 3

## *Can You Live Above Your Circumstances?*

My wife, Amy, knows about adversity. She was born in the Soviet Union under the reign of Lenin and Stalin, who ruled that nation through fear and terror. Historians estimate that during those years, approximately 60 million people died in labor camps, "purgings," and by systematic starvation.

During the years 1937 to 1941, these atrocities intensified as farmers, most of the intelligentsia, people who belonged to the wrong political party, individuals whose "crime" was that they had graduated from the university, and many Christian leaders were lined up for assassination or sent away to rot in the Russian labor camps. During this period, when Amy was 18 months old, her father was arrested and taken away to Siberia.

When Amy was six, the German Army invaded Ukraine and took control of her homeland. A year later, Amy, her mother, and her brother were taken by cattle car to Germany to work as slaves in a forced labor camp. After the Allied victory in Europe, the family hid from Russian officials for a year, fearing for their lives. Amy grew up in a foreign country without citizenship and without knowing her father. Her circumstances were definitely bleak for many years.

My wife told her story in her autobiography, *Goodbye Is Not Forever*. It is a story of great faith and hope. Amy's mother, Maria, was a wonderful mom to her children; she showed no bitterness about her lot in life. There were millions of people like her who suffered terribly during and after World War II. But not all people responded to their circumstances like Amy's mother. Since writing her story, Amy has received many letters from people whose parents or relatives had similar experiences but were never able to get over their anger, bitterness, and hatred. Their emotions consumed them for the rest of their lives.

How can one person emerge triumphant from tragedy and live above his or her circumstances, while another plunges into the depths of depression? The answer is surprisingly simple. The key is in our minds and the choices we make. A person must choose, under the stresses of life, which influence he or she will depend upon.

Man's mind can be programmed either by the world's philosophies or by truth, which is God's Word. It's up to us which influence we will depend upon when facing life's problems. If we rely on ourselves to change our circumstances, or we try to control our situations and the people around us, we will find ourselves on what I call the "downward spiral to depression."

## What Is Depression?

Before we see how we get depressed, let's make sure we understand what depression is. Depression is an emotional state of feeling sad, discouraged, and dejected or "down and out." There are many emotional symptoms that characterize a depressed state. Some of these might include:

- preoccupation with self
- fear and worry

- sadness
- loss of affection for others
- withdrawal from people and activities
- self-condemnation
- hopelessness
- at its worst, a desire to die

Sadness, even gloom, dominate a depressed person's perspective. Sometimes a person will disguise his or her depression by being sarcastic and tossing everything off with a joke. They use humor to mask their sadness. Others reveal their sadness by being touchy or on the verge of tears much of the time.

Left unchecked, such sadness turns into hostility. A depressed person will become irritable, especially towards those who are upbeat. In addition, depressed people either grow anxious about everything or become indifferent to the world around them.

Over time, these symptoms deepen. A depressed person may feel trapped in and by his circumstances. You might see this, for example, in a young couple who have their first baby nine months and one day after they get married. They had planned on spending time together doing fun things like traveling before they had family, but now the wife feels trapped by the baby. She loves her husband, but he's also the one to blame for her pregnancy. Her freedom is gone. That can produce ambivalence—she loves her husband but hates what has happened to her.

You can see this kind of ambivalence in other relationships: I may love my mother but hate being around her. I may like my boss yet I can't stand working for him. These kinds of situations sometimes lead to a state of hopelessness and confusion.

The emotions that come from such situations can ultimately lead a person to the point where he or she wishes to die. That is the final destination of an unchecked thinking habit called depression. Of course, a Christian is too embarrassed to say, "I feel like dying." So instead, he or she may mask his or her pain with statements like, "I wish the Lord would come back and take me home," or "I'm tired of living down here."

These emotional reactions may result in physical symptoms such as:

- self-abasing behavior (including no desire to eat or constant overeating)
- erratic sleep
- weight loss or gain
- apathy
- fatigue
- loss of sex drive
- illness

Sometimes depression is demonstrated through various channels of "escape," such as drug or alcohol abuse, sex, work, or fantasizing. In the latter category, delusion can eventually lead a person to believe he or she has

---

*Depression is never cured by treating the symptom (emotions); it's cured by treating the mind.*

---

committed the unpardonable sin. For example, when I was living in Southern California, my wife and I spent time working with women in a prison. Many of these women had no religious background, but they had all heard the term "unpardonable sin," and most of them were sure they had committed it. Everyone who thought that way was in a depressed state, feeling hopeless in their situation.

Of course, not all physical illnesses or symptoms are the result of depression. But if a number of the afore-mentioned physical symptoms are evident, consider depression as a possible underlying explanation.

As you can see, there are many symptoms of depression and they vary greatly among people. Because depression is basically an emotional problem, and emotions respond only to what we are thinking, depression is never cured by treating the symptom (emotions); it's cured by treating the mind.

## The Recipe for Depression

Depression is like a cake; it is made up of many ingredients. Just as it takes certain measures of flour, sugar, and eggs combined together to make a cake, it also takes several ingredients to create depression. These ingredients are illustrated in the following chart:

**IMPROPER THINKING PATTERNS**
Unrealistic Expectations and Misplaced Dependencies
▼

**REJECTION    INSULT    INJURY**
(Any adverse circumstance)
▼

**DISAPPOINTMENT**
▼

**FEAR/ANGER**
(Fleshly response to adverse circumstances)
▼

**SELF-PITY**
(Result of past/future thinking or fantasy)
▼

**DEPRESSION**
(Emotional state of feeling sad and dejected)
▼

**DESPAIR**

Note the progression. If you have ever experienced or suffered from depression, you will recognize some or perhaps even all the elements on this chart.

Although we may be totally unaware of this fact, depression always starts with improper thinking patterns made up of either unrealistic expectations or misplaced dependencies. We will learn more about this in chapters 4 and 5. When you experience the realities of life with all of its rejections, insults, and injuries and you are engaged in improper thinking, you set yourself up for disappointment.

The degree of disappointment you experience from an adverse circumstance is directly related to the level of your unrealistic expectations or misplaced dependencies. In other words, the more unrealistic expectations you have, the greater your hurt and disappointment will be. It is in this seedbed of disappointment that you have the choice to respond in such a way that will either protect you from depression or make you a candidate for it. When you choose to respond negatively to an adverse circumstance, you begin the downward spiral to depression. This anger can be aimed at God, a mate, a friend, an enemy, a boss, a parent, or anyone else. And whenever there is depression, there is always anger without exception, whether hidden or expressed.

## The Fear/Anger Connection

Tom's voice trembled with emotion as he told his story. The tension between him and his wife had been increasing for some time, with their arguments getting louder and more frequent. Yesterday was the last straw; she was leaving Tom unless he agreed to seek counsel.

"What can I do about my temper?" Tom asked. "I really do love Cindy, but for some reason I end up acting like a maniac around the house. Sometimes it is happening at work, too. I am afraid that eventually I could get fired for my behavior.

"I try so hard to control my anger, but I end up exploding anyway. I've confessed my problem to God many, many times and asked Him to forgive me, but nothing changes. What is the answer?"

I asked Tom a few questions to get more information about his situation, then told him something that surprised him: "Frankly, Tom, your real problem isn't anger. The reason that you are outwardly such an angry person is that, inwardly, you are a very fearful person. Your anger is a secondary response to deep-seated fear."

People usually react with surprise when I say this, and Tom was no exception. I have found fear to be the hidden root beneath a multitude of the outward problems people have.

"Here's an illustration to show you what I mean, Tom," I continued. "Let's say that you are walking down a street at night. I am a friend of yours who sees you from a distance and I decide to play a practical joke. I quickly hide behind a tree and then jump out at you with a loud growl as you pass by. What would be your first response?"

"Fear," Tom answered.

"Right, and when you see that it is just me, and I am collapsing in hysterical laughter at your reaction, what is your second response?"

"I'd probably want to kill you!"

"And," I continued, "how do you think you would respond if this happened over and over again?"

"I guess I would be fearful, angry, and jumpy just about all the time."

Tom was right: Fear is a paralyzing emotion. And a person who continuously lives in fear manifests it through being angry all the time.

If we fail to realize this, we will end up living in a futile cycle of trying to deal with the outward symptoms of anger without ever identifying the fears that are the root of our problem. It is like trying to rid your yard of weeds by merely pulling off their heads. If you leave the roots untouched, the weeds will grow back shortly.

Let's return to our chart on the progression of depression and consider another situation. If you are depending upon your spouse or any other person to make you happy, you will experience disappointment because he or she is not performing the way you want. That's when fear first arises. You'll become afraid as you think that perhaps this person will never make you happy. The fear that your needs might never be met will lead you to try to manipulate or to change that person. As your fear intensifies and your efforts to control that person fail, the natural result is frustration and anger. When you let these hidden feelings continue to eat away at you, then you naturally plunge into self-pity.

## The Bondage of Self-Pity

Seldom do the obvious problems and tragedies of the present time take us down the path to depression. We may be depressed for a short period of time in response to the loss of a loved one or a similar situation; that's a natural way of coping with such adversity. However, it is usually the multiplied insults, injuries, and rejections of our *past* that, when dwelled upon, lead us to the beginning of depression. Then we combine the hurts of the past with the insults, injuries, and rejections in our present, and then we complicate matters by projecting those hurts through our vivid fantasies into our future. As these fears and insecurities from continual disappointment begin to control us, we will respond in fear and anger.

Once fear and anger set in, we resort to using control mechanisms in an attempt to change our circumstances or to protect ourselves from further disappointment. Unfortunately, doing that doesn't work! The control mechanisms might accomplish a momentary gain, but ultimately, they never achieve their purpose. So the anger multiplies and festers into self-pity.

Self-pity, like anger, is an ingredient in all types of depression. The progression toward self-pity is as follows:

1. Discouragement, which results in anger and self-pity;

2. Despondency, which results in more self-pity;

3. Despair, which results in even more self-pity.

Self-pity means exactly what the word implies—a total preoccupation with feeling sorry for oneself.

Accompanied with an increase in self-pity is an increase in anger. When you discover that no one wants to join you in your pity party, you will become more aggravated and convince yourself that your depressed state of mind is justified. This, in turn, sets off negative thought patterns directed toward the past and future.

## The Path to Self-Pity

Here's how it works. I know you'd never do this, but let's suppose you just insulted me. In that one incident, you didn't treat me the way I wanted to be treated. Let's say that instead of forgiving you, I start mulling over the insult. This makes me more angry. Then I start thinking about the past and come to realize that you never have treated me the way I wanted to be treated over the years. Now instead of having one angry incident, I have more to think about. Then let's say that I think not only about how you have mistreated me, but how my mother used to mistreat me. Now I have a collection of hurts in my mind. Then I add to that the memories about my fifth-grade teacher, who didn't treat me right either. Now I don't know how many incidents I have to think about, but it's a bunch! And if that isn't enough, I start looking into the future. I begin to speculate that you will never treat me right. You'll probably be insulting me all the way to the grave. Things will never change!

The more I think those kinds of thoughts, the angrier I will become. And soon I will be wallowing in self-pity. "Woe is me, nobody ever treats me right. Nobody ever treated me right. Nobody will ever treat me right." I've let my very depressing thoughts lead to some very depressing emotions.

A person immersed in self-pity usually develops unrealistic attitudes and says, "God is against me. The whole world is against me. No one is on my side." Or, "I'm nothing but a failure. I've always been a failure. I will always be a failure." Like a recording, the mind keeps on playing: "Nothing is going my way. Nothing will ever go my way."

---

*The Bible addresses
every ingredient that makes up
depression!*

---

The more deeply you indulge in self-pity, the more depressed you will become. Until self-pity is confronted and arrested, a person will never be able to live above his or her circumstances. Self-pity keeps a person trapped in a cycle of improper thinking patterns and undesirable emotional responses. All of this results in depression, which, if not corrected, will ultimately lead to an attitude of despair or hopelessness.

## Overcoming Depression

Can you live above your circumstances and avoid the pathway to depression? The answer is an overwhelming, *yes!*

A number of years ago I appeared on a television broadcast along with Dr. Joyce Brothers to discuss depression. The interviewer asked me why, in my ministry, I concentrated on helping people with depression. "Because" I explained, "no one ever comes for counseling unless they are depressed over their circumstances." It's not until we learn how to deal with depression that we'll learn how to live above the difficult circumstances of life, no matter what they are.

Depression is not a wanted or pleasant emotion. No one likes to feel depressed. When someone comes in for counseling, they want to hear something that will make them *feel* better. However, true biblical counseling should concentrate on how to make people *think* better.

The key point is that *depression, for everyone, begins in the mind with improper thinking patterns.* The issue is, how do we change these damaging thinking patterns and thoughts? I assure you that if your foundation is on Christ and His Word, you can find an answer to that question and freedom from depression. The Bible addresses every ingredient that makes up depression. Christ, in His Word, provides answers to our improper thinking patterns: He gives us the solution to fear, He tells us how to handle anger, and points us to His love, forgiveness, and mercy so we do not have to wallow in self-pity. Over the last 20 years I have taught these biblical truths and seen thousands of people set free. If you are reading this book and are depressed because of your circumstances, I believe that you, too, can experience freedom. Just as we have learned how depression starts in the mind, victory over it begins there, too.

# 4

## Dealing with Unrealistic Expectations

Amy and I met in Germany when I was in the Army. We were married there and spent our honeymoon in Rome, Italy. Rome was like Disneyland to me. I had studied its history all through high school. Latin was my favorite subject, and I was even the president of the Latin Club. The thought of standing in the Coliseum or seeing the Sistine Chapel sent chills up my spine. So, the opportunity to visit Rome during our honeymoon was, for me, the thrill of a lifetime.

The first place we visited was the Coliseum. There it was, just as I had pictured it. My heart was racing with excitement. I now could walk down the steps and stand in the same place where the early Christians were fed to the lions. Instead of walking, however, I *ran* down the steps as fast as I could to experience this sense of history!

For some reason, Amy wasn't right behind me. I looked up and she was still standing at the top of the steps. I urged her to come down, but she refused.

It had rained that day and there were puddles of water and some mud on the Coliseum floor. Amy didn't want to join me because she was concerned about ruining her new shoes. *That's ridiculous,* I thought. I wanted us to enjoy this special occasion together. Here I was standing in the center of one of the most historical places in the world while Amy waited for me from a distance. That was not how I expected this moment to be. I had assumed that Amy would be as thrilled to see the Coliseum as I was. But I was disappointed!

What made matters worse was that I didn't understand why she was so concerned about her shoes. The fact is, Amy's background and childhood was totally different from mine. She grew up in a small village in Ukraine during the war years. Her father was taken from the family and shipped to the frigid wastelands of Siberia. Amy's mom was left to provide and care for the family as best as she could. Material possessions were hard to come by. During the winters, Amy spent her time indoors because she didn't have shoes to wear. On one occasion, her mom traded some dried fruit for a pair of winter boots for Amy.

For Amy's family, then, shoes were very special and had to be taken care of. The family could not afford a new pair as needed or purchase different pairs of shoes to match different outfits. Everyone had to make their shoes last as long as possible.

In contrast, when I grew up, if you got your shoes dirty, you bought a new pair. So, here was the conflict.

The shoes Amy wore on that day in Rome were special to her. She certainly didn't want to ruin them at the beginning of our honeymoon. Of course, she expected me to understand that. As a result, she got angry at me, and I got angry at her. What I thought would be one of the most memorable highlights of our honeymoon turned out to be our first fight as a married couple.

Today, as I look back on that incident, I see how both of us approached that moment with unrealistic expectations about each other. In my mind, Amy was supposed to be as caught up in the history of Rome as I was. And she just knew I would understand and be sympathetic to all of her desires and concerns. When this circumstance did not turn out the way we thought it should and we didn't live up to each other's expectations, we got angry at each other.

## A Candid Look at Our Human Nature

Like our emotions, unrealistic expectations toward life and other people aren't unusual. We come into this world with the idea that everything and everyone is here to make us happy. By nature, we are self-centered.

Let me illustrate this for you. Have you ever watched a little baby for long? It will soon become apparent to you that the baby seems to think he is the center of the universe. Everyone around him is there to serve and meet all of his needs. When a baby wakes up in the middle of the night hungry, he doesn't think to himself, "Mommy is probably sleepy and tired, so I'll wait until morning to get fed so she can get a little more sleep." No, he screams and yells until someone comes in and takes care of him.

As we grow up, we are taught the concepts of sharing and getting along with others, but our human nature is still bent toward self-centeredness. If we are honest with ourselves, we will confess that we generally think of ourselves as important persons whose needs and desires should take precedence over others. Paul gives an accurate description of this perception in Ephesians 2:1-3:

> As for you, you were dead in your transgressions and sins, in which you used to live when you followed the ways of this world and of the ruler of the kingdom of the air, the spirit who is now at work in those who are disobedient. All of us also lived among them at one time, gratifying the cravings of our [flesh] and following its desires and thoughts.

Our natural pattern for living is to follow the desires and thoughts of our sinful flesh and to follow the ways of this world and the ruler of the kingdom of the air. Our basic human nature does not follow God's way, nor does it follow God's thoughts. In fact, the prophet Isaiah tells us, "'For my thoughts are not your thoughts, neither are your ways my ways,' declares the Lord" (Isaiah 55:8).

So, it is not unusual for us to approach life with thoughts that do not match up with God's thoughts. We all have improper thinking patterns. I thought improperly toward Amy that day in Rome, and she towards me.

After many years of counseling with people, I have come to realize that our improper thinking patterns fall into one of two categories. I have already introduced one to you—unrealistic expectations. The other category is misplaced dependencies. Understanding these two areas of our thinking is critical to learning how to live above our circumstances. Let's take a look at each one more closely, both here and in the next chapter.

## A Survey of Unrealistic Expectations

Unrealistic expectations arise when we don't face life as it really is, but instead look at life and people as we think they *should* be. Notice that I said, "As we *think* they *should* be."

We have seen from previous chapters that the way we *think* influences how we feel and behave. When we think, or expect, a circumstance to be one way or people to act a certain way, we will always be disappointed. Circumstances do not always turn out the way we think they should, and people do not always act the way we think they should.

When we go through life thinking unrealistically, we buy into Satan's lie. We will believe a false reality that will always let us down. An example of this would be when I attended my 25-year class reunion. I went there expecting everyone to still look the same as when we were in high school. How sobering it was to see that my classmates had aged significantly since the last time I saw them!

Let's go on now and identify some major kinds of unrealistic expectations and see how they affect us.

***Everyone should like me.*** This unrealistic expectation starts early in life. Many of us grow up hearing our parents, relatives, or friends say, "You are the cutest thing in the world. You have the best personality." This may eventually cause us to think, *since I am the cutest person in the world, who is not going to like me?* Most of the time, this bubble bursts on the first day of school.

But children aren't the only ones who fall prey to this line of thinking. I see it in adults as well—especially ministers. Ministers enter the ministry hoping that everyone will love and respect them. Who wouldn't love and respect someone who has devoted his life to serving God and others? Yet many have left the ministry when they were confronted with the painful reality of Jesus' words, "If they persecuted me, they will persecute you also" (John 15:20).

Whether you are a child or an adult, reality says that not everyone is going to like you, and you are not going to like everyone in return.

***Life will always be good.*** This one isn't always outwardly expressed, but oftentimes it is inwardly assumed. In fact, most of us would intellectually agree that life *isn't* always good. But picture, if you will, someone hoping to win the lottery. The person thinks, *If only I had enough money, I could have anything I want. Indeed, life would then be good.* Or would it?

We sometimes wish that God would exempt us from bad times. And when bad things happen, we become discouraged and depressed. We may not want to admit it, but deep down we generally expect life to be good.

*He or she can bring me happiness.* Many people enter marriage or a new relationship with this thought: "Here I am, just a bundle of needs. Have at it; make me happy!" This again is a perfect picture of the self-centeredness I mentioned earlier. When your spouse or partner doesn't make you happy, or fails to meet one of your needs, you go into action, tell him or her about it, and set out to make sure it doesn't happen again. Of course, this puts more stress on the relationship. And if you both do this, then you both become like a tick on a dog, sucking the very life out of each other. It is no wonder that relationships crumble and one out of every two marriages end in divorce! This attitude of demanding from each other is the exact opposite of what the apostle Paul speaks of in Galatians 5:13: "Serve one another in love."

---

*As Christians, our peace of mind comes from standing on the solid rock— Jesus Christ.*

---

*I can be secure in this world.* Years ago, a television commercial guaranteed viewers peace of mind if they had a "piece of the rock." The company promoting this concept urged people to buy insurance to protect themselves against any "unforeseen circumstance."

As Christians, our peace of mind comes from standing on the solid rock—Jesus Christ. Trusting in riches, insurance, or any other material resource that we believe will make us secure is false security.

*Ambitions of independence.* This unrealistic expectation is one that is frequently preceded by the words, "If only...":

"If only I had a car; then I could do anything I wanted."
"If only I had my own business and was my own boss."
"If only I was out of this marriage."

This way of thinking is also known as the greener-grass mentality. The circumstance you *are not* in looks more attractive, and you want to be free to explore the "other side" of the fence. The only problem with going after the greener grass is that once you are standing in it, the weeds are magnified!

***My children are perfect.*** If you are even thinking about your children being perfect, you are destined for deep disappointment. The reason children are not perfect is...well, because we as parents are not perfect. Like us, our children also have a sin nature. So, why expect anything different?

Accepting this truth is difficult for most parents. We can accept it about other people's children, but not with our own. This is why so many parents take their children to counselors today. Mom assumes that because little Johnny is basically good, there has to be some external reason that he misbehaves, or can't pay attention in class, or is constantly fidgeting. Of course, some counselors would like you to believe that this kind of behavior is abnormal, even though it isn't. In case you have forgotten, children naturally act this way. They act this way because, by nature, all are indwelled by sin.

***Quick fixes to problems.*** This is a major expectation in our society. If something is broken, we expect it to be repaired now. If we're ill, we expect a prescription that will relieve the symptoms immediately. If we have a problem in a relationship, it has to be smoothed over right away. We are impatient people. When we don't get a quick result, we frequently get angry and miserable.

---

*The good news
for Christians is that we don't have to
yield to our old desires. They no longer
have power over us.*

---

**My old desires will eventually go away.** Some Christians expect that either after salvation or with time, their old sinful desires will disappear, never to return. After all, we have been crucified with Christ. So isn't our flesh dead? No, it isn't! To expect our sinful desires to go away is a prescription for continuous disappointment. Yes, God has given us a new nature—His nature—but our flesh will not go away until we die and are in the presence of Jesus. The good news for Christians is not that our old desires will disappear, but that we don't have to yield to them. They no longer have power over us.

**A real Christian would never do that.** We usually have high expectations of our fellow believers and of ourselves. For example, we know that the mark of a Christian is love. Thus, we assume that Christians will always love each other. We don't expect non-Christians to act in a loving way, so we generally aren't disappointed when they don't. But what happens when a Christian lies to us, steals, gossips, or double-crosses us? We feel the hurt much more deeply, and we tend to get angry. This is what I refer to as the *Christian Phantom Syndrome.*

The Christian Phantom Syndrome is our tendency to think there is this ideal Christian somewhere who does everything right. He has his life together. His marriage is constant bliss. His children are well-behaved, do well in school, and stay out of trouble. We set ourselves up for disappointment when we compare ourselves and everyone else to this unrealistic standard. When we see a Christian brother or sister fall into an unfortunate situation, we may say things like, "I can't believe they did that!" Or, "I am so disappointed in him or her"—all because we hold to the unrealistic expectation that Christians are supposed to be perfect.

Christianity is not about how well we behave but who we are in Christ. If we could act perfectly, why would we need Jesus? He is the only perfect One. That is why we live by faith in Him and His perfection.

---

*Christianity is not about how well
we behave but who we are
in Christ.*

---

Don't be surprised, then, when you see someone make a mistake. That person did so because he still lives in the flesh like we all do. As long as we live in this world, we have indwelling sin attached to us. Why should we be surprised when Christians don't always act appropriately?

***Confidence in the flesh.*** The apostle Paul addresses this expectation in Romans 7:14-25:

> We know that the law is spiritual; but I am unspiritual, sold as a slave to sin. I do not understand what I do. For what I want to do I do not do, but what I hate I do. And if I do what I do not want to do, I agree that the law is good. As it is, it is no longer I myself who do it, but it is sin living in me. I know that nothing good lives in me, that is, in my sinful nature. For I have the desire to do what is good, but I cannot carry it out.

For what I do is not the good I want to do; no, the evil I do not want to do—this I keep on doing. Now if I do what I do not want to do, it is no longer I who do it, but it is sin living in me that does it.

So I find this law at work: When I want to do good, evil is right there with me. For in my inner being I delight in God's law; but I see another law at work in the members of my body, waging war against the law of my mind and making me a prisoner of the law of sin at work within my members. What a wretched man I am! Who will rescue me from this body of death? Thanks be to God— through Jesus Christ our Lord!

Have you ever experienced the kind of inner turmoil Paul talks about? The things I want to do I don't do. And the things I don't want to do I do them anyway. Notice Paul didn't say, "What a wretched man I am, and it's all my parents' fault." He didn't blame the fact he was single or that he'd suffered all kinds of unpleasant circumstances. He merely confirmed what Christ said: "Apart from Me you can do nothing" (John 15:5).

Anytime we think we can do something good apart from the power of Christ within us, we are setting ourselves up for disappointment. Scripture says that in our flesh is no good thing. The deeds of the flesh are listed in Galatians 5:19-20—sexual immorality, impurity, hatred, discord, jealousy, fits of rage, selfish ambition, dissensions, factions, envy, and so on. Only the Holy Spirit, who indwells a believer, can produce what we really desire: love, joy, peace, patience, kindness, goodness, faithfulness, gentleness, and self-control (Galatians 5:22-23).

## Seeing Things God's Way

Maintaining an unrealistic view of life will doom us to living in constant disappointment. The more unrealistic our expectations, the greater our disappointment will be when we face reality.

If we want to develop realistic expectations about life, we must be open to seeing the world from God's perspective rather than our own. He sees things as they really are. He can teach us how to view life realistically so that we don't set ourselves up to be let down.

So many Christians today are struggling, living in self-effort, trying to accomplish what God says is already finished. God created us with a need to be dependent. If we are not dependent upon *Him,* we will be forced, of necessity, to look elsewhere to fulfill this need.

Having completed our look at dealing with unrealistic expectations, let's now turn our attention to correcting misplaced dependencies.

# 5

## *Correcting Misplaced Dependencies*

Misplaced dependencies result when a person depends upon someone or something other than God for his or her happiness, self-worth, or meaning in life. Misplaced dependencies naturally follow unrealistic expectations. For instance, if you expect your spouse to make you happy and to meet all your needs, then you will naturally depend upon him or her for your happiness.

If you are married, I hope that you know by now that your spouse will never be able to fill the void in your life. (Pay attention, newlyweds!) The reason is simple: Your spouse is a created being just as you are, and both of you have needs. No human being can love another unconditionally. This can only be experienced in a spiritual relationship with God because it is a spiritual need. When we experience His unconditional love we take the pressure off our spouse to meet that need, and only then can we enjoy each other

Dependency is not bad when it is placed on the proper object—God. As I have explained, you and I were created by God to depend upon Him. If we are not going to depend upon Christ—who is the only One able to satisfy our deepest needs for our happiness, self-worth, and meaning in life—we will, of necessity, depend upon something or someone else.

Whenever you depend upon someone else for the things only God can provide, you put them under stress to perform. A human being, however, cannot take the place of God. Also, whenever you depend upon others—or things—for meaning and purpose in life, eventually you will succumb to their control.

## A Survey of Misplaced Dependencies

Let's take a look now at some examples of misplaced dependencies and how they control our lives.

*Money.* It seems like most of our problems relate to money matters. How many of us feel that we could use just a little more money? We think if only we had a little more, we'd be happy and secure. But how much is enough?

Nelson Rockefeller answered the question of how much money would be enough for him by saying, "Just a little more." In other words, there is never an end to our desires. We constantly look for a little more.

*Drugs and alcohol.* A 1993 National Household Survey of Drug Abuse reported that both men and women were abusing drugs at an alarming rate. According to the study, teenage girls under 18 are now just as likely to smoke, drink, and use drugs as teenage boys of the same age. In other age groups, women were quickly closing the gaps.

Mankind has certainly wandered far from his dependency upon his Creator! If we don't come to our senses, our society's dependency upon drugs and alcohol could destroy the whole nation.

*Appearance and talent.* Every now and then on television, we see commercials praising the benefits of cosmetic surgery. A nip and a tuck and you can look like a model. Or, you will look years younger! The sad truth is, models worry even more about their looks than the average person because they are in such a short-lived and competitive occupation.

Or, what about professional athletes in our society? They are fast becoming the primary role models for our children simply because they have outstanding talent. What happens when they get too old to perform, or they get injured or disabled? There is nothing that sounds worse to an athlete than to be an "ex" whose total self-worth was wrapped up in performance.

---

*Your true identity*
*comes from God and how He sees you—*
*not from how the world treats you.*

---

It is natural for us to think that the more beautiful a person is physically, or the more talented a person is, the greater the success he or she will enjoy, which supposedly results in happiness and fulfillment. Good looks and talent are nice if you have them, but if you put your total identity and dependency upon those temporary attributes, you will live a life of striving and disappointment.

***Job or career.*** I've known people who have totally given themselves to their job or career. For a while, I was one of them.

Interestingly, surveys have shown that most people are unhappy with their work and the way they have to make a living. Most men, and some women, have a high expectation that a job should provide satisfaction and meaning to life. In contrast, for those who love their work, there is always the lurking fear of losing their job. And if for some reason they *are* fired, retired, or laid off, they often go through severe depression because their self-worth was wrapped up in their work.

Let me say here that, as a child of God, what you *do* is not who you *are*. Your true identity comes from God and how He sees you—not from how the world treats you.

***"Spiritual" experiences or feelings.*** This misplaced dependency is often seen in the Body of Christ. It's seen in believers who feel that spiritual experiences are signs from God or assurances of His love and acceptance... endorsements of true spirituality. For them, it is not enough that God's love was demonstrated to us through His work on the cross. They look for more signs to assure them of God's presence.

Of course, this is nothing new. People were looking for similar signs back in the days of Jesus. When He overturned the tables of the money changers in the Temple, the Jews demanded a sign from Him to prove His authority to take such actions. He answered them, "Destroy this temple, and I will raise it again in three days" (John 2:19). They did not realize He was referring to His death, burial, and resurrection.

On a different occasion the Pharisees were again disturbed by Jesus' words, so they demanded a sign: "Teacher, we want to see a miraculous sign from you" (Matthew 12:38).

Jesus had some harsh words for them: "A wicked and adulterous generation asks for a miraculous sign! But none will be given it except the sign of the prophet Jonah. For as Jonah was three days and three nights in the belly of a huge fish, so the Son of Man will be three days and three nights in the heart of the earth" (Matthew 12:39-40).

Jesus pointed the Pharisees to His death, burial, and resurrection, which they would witness with their own eyes. They would see Him die at the hands of the Romans, witness His body being placed in the grave, plead with the Roman officials to place a huge stone in front of the tomb and keep a guard posted outside day and night, then observe His resurrection from the dead. There is nothing quite so miraculous as someone being raised from the dead.

If the Pharisees could not believe that Jesus was who He claimed to be and put their faith in Him after witnessing His resurrection, why would they believe any other sign or miracle? The same is true with us. If we are not willing to accept Christ's work on our behalf through His death, burial, and resurrection, why would we believe any other miracle? Asking for signs is nothing more than a preoccupation with miracles rather than Jesus—a preoccupation with gifts rather than the gift-Giver. Sooner or later this will lead to disappointment and spiritual burnout.

---

*Christ, by His sacrifice,
can now present you holy in His sight,
without blemish, totally free
from any accusation.*

---

***Trying to perfect ourselves.*** One misplaced dependency many people have is that of thinking it is their responsibility to make themselves perfect. We expect perfection of ourselves and others. When we or others don't match up to our expectations, we try to make improvements. Yet this is nothing more than trying to control our circumstances, which results in a life of total frustration. The good news is that the perfection we desire has been given to us by faith through Christ. You don't have to try to make yourself perfect anymore. You are already perfect forever!

That's the message of Hebrews 10:14: "By one sacrifice He has made perfect forever those who are being made holy." Christ, by His sacrifice, can now present you holy in His sight, without blemish, totally free from any accusation. When Jesus said upon the cross, "It is finished," He meant it! When something is finished, it is complete.

Let's suppose that during a trip to Paris I decide to tour the Louvre Museum. While walking through I see Leonardo Da Vinci's *Mona Lisa*. I'm so moved by this masterpiece that I buy it on the spot for millions and millions of dollars. I carefully ship it back home to my personal art studio. As I look at the painting I start to think, "Maybe I can make this painting a little better." So, I set it up on an easel, get out my paint, and begin dabbling on the *Mona Lisa*, trying to improve it. But there is no way I can make this masterpiece better. The minute I add something of my own to Da Vinci's work, I rob it of its value. The master's work is perfect as it is. There is nothing more I could do to improve the painting. Of course, the art world would think I had lost my mind if I attempted to do something like that.

In the same way, no one in their right mind would pull out a chisel to improve Michelangelo's *David*. No one would try and rewrite a symphony by Beethoven. These are the works of masters. They are meant to be enjoyed just as they are, and any effort on our part to improve on these would only cheapen the finished works of the masters.

When it comes to the finished work of Jesus, oftentimes we pull out our paints and try to improve on it. Yet there is nothing more we can add through our self-efforts to improve on what He has done. He has already done it all. Because of His sacrifice, we are perfect and complete forever.

***Trying to perfect others.*** What happens when we discover that people don't match up to our expectations? What happens when the things we are depending upon for happiness or self-worth let us down?

Let me share a story with you that will help you to understand the ultimate danger of unrealistic expectations and misplaced dependencies.

One day we received a call from a woman requesting help for her problem with anger. It didn't take long for Joan to express how angry she was at several of her Christian friends. They were not treating her like she thought they should. They weren't mean to her or unkind; they just weren't doing enough.

What was Joan's problem? She had a mental image of how Christians should behave and respond. Joan wanted her group of friends to be like those Luke described in Acts 4:32-33: "All the believers were one in heart and mind. No one claimed that any of his possessions was his own, but they shared everything they had . . . There were no needy persons among them."

When Joan had a need, she wanted her friends to drop everything and respond to her immediately. Interestingly, it didn't bother Joan when these ladies didn't respond quickly to the needs of others. She was angry because they weren't paying attention to *her*. On top of that, Joan claimed she was always willing to go the extra mile for them.

Joan's response to her situation wasn't unusual. She, like many of us, had unrealistic expectations towards others, and, as a result, she had misplaced dependencies. Joan was simply displaying our basic human nature. The problem is *where* these unrealistic expectations and misplaced dependencies can lead us if we don't recognize improper thinking patterns.

One of the problems Joan experienced came from comparing herself to her friends. "If I am this way, why aren't they?" she asked. In other words, she had established herself as the standard instead of realizing that every person alive is different in their own way from other people. Just as we look different, so also do we think and act differently. We have to accept this reality of life and be willing to overlook what we think are shortcomings, just as we would want other people to overlook what they perceive as our shortcomings.

Jesus put it this way: "Do not judge, or you too will be judged" (Matthew 7:1). How can we judge others for their imperfections when we have imperfections as well? Have you ever noticed that when you point a finger at someone, you have three fingers pointing back at you? That is why Jesus went on to say, "First take the plank out of your own eye, and then you will see clearly to remove the speck from your brother's eye" (Matthew 7:5).

We are all under construction. God is completing His work in each and every one of us. So instead of condemning or judging others, we are to reach out to them with an attitude of restoration. When we see someone straying off the straight and narrow, we can respond with the same attitude expressed in Galatians 6:1: "Brothers, if someone is caught in a sin, you who are spiritual should restore him gently. But watch yourself, or you also may be tempted."

When we judge or compare ourselves to others, there are only two things that can happen, and both are bad.

First, you may end up thinking you are better than others, which is pride. Or, you may start thinking you are worse than others, which is self-condemnation. Neither option is desirable. Comparing ourselves to others leads us to live with the world's perspective rather than God's.

Joan wanted her friends to be more like her, willing to go that extra mile. When her friends didn't live up to her expectations, she tried to change them. The harder she tried, the less they responded. That was what made her so mad. This cycle of thinking had to be broken, or she could lapse into severe depression.

Had Joan continued in that mindset, she would have headed for problems much bigger than her disappointment with friends. Fortunately, I was able to help Joan with her unrealistic expectations and misplaced dependencies, which were causing her to try to control and manipulate her friends and situations.

***Making ourselves acceptable to God before He will answer our prayers.*** There is an incredible promise in Hebrews 4:16. There, we read that because of who we are in Christ, we can approach God's throne with confidence and receive mercy and grace in our time of need. Hebrews 10:19 says that we can enter the most holy place, with confidence, by the blood of Jesus Christ. Do you really understand what that means? Because of who we are in Christ, you and I can go into the presence of God with confidence. We can walk up to His throne and call him, "Abba, Father." Or, as we might say, "Daddy, Daddy!" like a small child calling to a loving Father.

Unfortunately, most of us approach God like the prodigal son. The son demanded his inheritance, went away, and squandered it all. Later, when he was broke, he got a job feeding pigs. He was so hungry he would have eaten the pigs' food. In the midst of all that, no one cared about him.

When he came to his senses and realized that his father's servants were living better than he was, he prepared a speech for his dad, saying that he had sinned against him. He hoped that his dad would take him back and make him one of his servants. The prodigal son forgot who he was and who he belonged to! As you know, the father was overjoyed to see his son return home, and welcomed him with open arms.

Even though we may mess up in life and find ourselves, as Hebrews 4:16 states, "in our time of need," we can still go boldly into God's presence because we are children of God and have been clothed in Christ's righteousness. We don't have to prepare a speech or bargain with God. We are His children. When we go boldly to Him, we can be confident that we'll be greeted with open and loving arms—just as the prodigal son was.

Many people feel they aren't worthy enough to go into God's presence. Maybe you feel that way. I've got news for you: I'm not worthy either. That is, I'm not worthy because of anything I have done. No one can approach God on their own merits. But I *am* worthy because I am clothed in the righteousness of the worthy One. I have the privilege of going to the throne of God and calling Him *Father*. You have the same privilege!

## The Key to Change

After years of counseling, I have dealt with depressed thinking more than I care to write about. Always at the root of the problem are unrealistic expectations and misplaced dependencies. We've named only a few of each, but I trust that by now you are equipped to watch for destructive thought patterns in your own life. The good news is, there *is* a remedy. We can deal with unrealistic expectations and correct misplaced dependencies...by having our minds renewed by truth, which is God's Word.

# 6
## The Battle for Control

My associate, Bob Christopher, came into my office and asked if we could talk for a minute. He had just received a telephone call from a friend. Bob said that he could barely understand him over the receiver; he sounded like he was drunk and seemed as if he might even be suicidal. We immediately left the office and jumped into my car to go help Jim.

When we reached Jim's home, the door was unlocked and we walked in. It was dark inside, which was quite a contrast to the bright sunny day in Texas. The house reeked of vomit and cigarettes, and everything was in disarray. It wasn't a pretty sight. Suddenly a wrenching sound told us where he was. We walked down the hallway and found him in the bathroom on his knees, hugging the toilet. As he looked toward us, he moaned, "Help me. Help me... I'm out of control!"

After cleaning him up the best we could, we loaded him into the car and headed to the hospital. As I drove, his words pounded in my mind: "Help me... I'm out of control." As I pondered his statement, I wondered, *Is this really true? Is man ever* out *of control?*

My heart was saddened as I considered the reality that each of us are in a battle every day of our lives against an enemy whose only goal is our destruction. Jim felt that he was *out* of control because he was no longer *in* control of his drinking habit. Yet the truth is that no one is really *out* of control. Neither is anyone *in* control. Rather, every person is *under* the control of either God or Satan.

Why is this so?

## Dependent or Independent?

You and I were created to be dependent; however, we would like to think of ourselves as self-sufficient. God created us to live in dependency upon Him and His provision to meet every need we have. Jesus explained this truth in His illustration of the vine and the branch. In John 15:5, He said, "I am the vine; you are the branches. If a man remains in Me and I in him, he will bear much fruit; apart from Me you can do nothing." Christ is the vine, and we are the branches. The only way we can bear fruit is by living in total dependency upon the vine, because apart from Him, we can do nothing.

---

*God designed us in such a way that our needs can be met only through a dependent relationship with Him.*

---

God is the only One who is self-sufficient. He is totally independent. Paul affirms this fact in Acts 17:24-25: "The God who made the world and everything in it is the Lord of heaven and earth and does not live in temples built by hands. And He is not served by human hands, as if He needed anything, because He Himself gives all men life and breath and everything else." God gives; we receive.

As a branch, man cannot live independent of the vine. He needs the sustaining life that flows from God in order to survive.

Our basic needs, which are unique to our humanity, illustrate this point. God created us with a body, soul, and spirit. On each of these levels, we have needs that must be met for us to live and survive. The fact that we call these *needs* means we must look to a source outside of ourselves to have them met. God designed us in such a way that these needs can be met only through a dependent relationship with Him.

For example, on the physical level, we could not survive if we were not dependent upon the air we breathe, the food we eat, and the water we drink. As for the soul, it is made up of our mind, emotion, and will. Its needs are to be met through people, places, and things that are all part of God's creation. When we deny our soul's needs, we slowly wither inwardly and eventually turn into an unresponsive human being. Prisoners of war who have endured solitary confinement testify to this fact. It is also borne out through the many stories of orphans who have experienced isolation from human contact.

Spiritually, we have need for unconditional love, acceptance, and meaning and purpose in life. These are the deepest needs of the human heart. God created us in such a way that He alone can meet those needs. If we do not depend upon Him to fulfill those needs, we will search endlessly for people or things to do for us what only God can do.

## The Relationship Between Dependency and Control

Why is this issue of dependency so important? Because most of us do not realize that what we continually depend upon for our meaning to life will ultimately control us.

For years I depended upon my business for my well-being and self-worth. I counted success by the size of my warehouse, the sales I achieved each month, and the people I associated with and their opinions. I depended upon my business and, as a result, my business controlled me. The sad part was that my business did not even know me.

We see this in many areas of life. People depend upon drugs or alcohol to fill a void and find happiness. What eventually happens to them? Drugs and alcohol begin to control their lives. In marriage, if you depend upon your spouse to give you unconditional love and acceptance, your spouse will control you. Remember:

> *Whoever or whatever you depend upon*
> *will ultimately control you.*

A young woman called *People to People* one night to talk about her struggle with compulsive eating. "My mind is obsessed with food," Cheryl complained. But deeper than her obsession with food was her obsession with herself, her appearance, her fear of being fat. Many people don't like the way they look; it can consume their thinking and become a preoccupation.

Cheryl admitted that by her outward appearance few people would guess she had a problem with binge eating. Sadly, this is a hidden problem many women have. A traumatic event can cause the onset of this obsession. In Cheryl's case, when she was seven years old, she was sexually assaulted. "I swore to myself at that time that I would never be out of control again. It became so important to me to be in control of myself and not to become vulnerable or dependent on anyone or anything."

At first, Cheryl thought she could control her eating habit, but eventually, after trying and failing, she realized that she couldn't. No matter how many times she promised herself that she would never overeat again, she could not stay in control. Her eating disorder was evidence of that fact. When I talked to Cheryl about her problem, I referred her back to the Garden of Eden. I have always said that if you want to know what the source of something really is, you have to go back to where it began. In Genesis 3:1-6, we see where sin entered the world:

> Now the serpent was more crafty than any of the wild animals the LORD God had made. He said to the woman, "Did God really say, 'You must not eat from any tree in the garden'?" The woman said to the serpent, "We may eat fruit from the trees in the garden, but God did say, 'You must not eat fruit from the tree that is in the middle of the garden, and you must not touch it, or you will die.'
>
> "You will not surely die," the serpent said to the woman. "For God knows that when you eat of it your eyes will be opened, and you will be like God, knowing good and evil." When the woman saw that the fruit of the tree was good for food and pleasing to the eye, and also desirable for gaining wisdom, she took some and ate it. She also gave some to her husband, who was with her, and he ate it.

Satan had a good plan of attack set in place. By asking the question, "Did God really say...?" he cast doubt on what God had said to Adam. Then he questioned God's motive in forbidding Adam and Eve to eat from the tree of the knowledge of good and evil when he stated, "God knows that when you eat of it your eyes will be opened, and you will be like God."

Satan's ultimate goal in tempting Adam and Eve was to convince them that they could be like God. He wanted them to believe his lie and declare their independence from God.

After being convinced by Satan that they could be like God and determine what was good and evil without consulting Him, Adam and Eve declared their independence. Little did they know that independence from God meant living in dependency upon Satan. His lie would now control their lives.

The same plan that Satan used in the Garden of Eden is still in place today. It hasn't changed. His strategy has always been to control and destroy mankind—or, at best, paralyze Christians in their effectiveness.

Adam and Eve were not the first to fall, however. Satan had already fallen from his heavenly throne. Let's look at Isaiah 14:12-15 which records the scene:

> How you have fallen from heaven, O morning star, son of the dawn! You have been cast down to the earth, you who once laid low the nations! You said in your heart, I will ascend to heaven; I will raise my throne above the stars of God; I will sit enthroned on the mount of assembly, on the utmost heights of the sacred mountain. I will ascend above the tops of the clouds; I will make myself like the Most High. But you are brought down to the grave, to the depths of the pit.

Satan was not content to be what God created him to be. He wanted to rule—to be in control—rather than submit to God. He became puffed up with pride and tried to make himself like the Most High.

This explanation helped Cheryl to see that the essence of sin is the desire to be like God—that is, the desire to control things. You may wonder how God and control are connected. Well, what does God do? He controls the universe. This is what Satan wanted to do, and this is what Cheryl wanted to do in her limited circumstances. She wanted to control all of it: her destiny, how she looked, and her past, present and future so that no one could ever hurt her again. What we fail to understand, however, is that no one controls himself. When we refuse to let God control us, the remaining option is not that we run things ourselves, but that we fall under the control of another influence—the enemy of our soul.

A good way to illustrate this concept of control is to consider the laws of gravity and aerodynamics. Once an airplane takes off, everyone on board is under the control of the law of aerodynamics. If you should decide at 33,000 feet that you are tired of being in that plane and want to go outside for a walk, you will immediately find yourself under the control of gravity. There is never a time when you can avoid being under the control of one or the other.

The same is true with God and Satan. We are controlled by one or the other. Yet Satan has conned many people into believing a lie—that they can be in control of themselves. In Cheryl's case, Satan knew that if he could get her to think she needed to get in control of her life, he could continue to speak to her and make her think that her thoughts originated from her own mind. Satan always speaks to a person in his or her own voice; he is a master deceiver.

Cheryl, then, could never control herself—and neither can we. The very moment we decide not to let God control us, we fall into the control of Satan.

This truth about Satan and control applies to both Jim and Cheryl. Their problems were much deeper than drinking too much or binge eating. According to Jesus, they had a heart problem: "It's not what a man puts in his mouth that defiles a man, but what proceeds out of his heart" (see Matthew 15:17-18). So you see, in both cases, what they were putting into their mouth, either alcohol or food, was not the problem. The problem was that in their hearts, they were believing Satan's lie. As long as they tried to solve either their eating disorder or their drinking problem, they were dealing with the outward symptom and not the inward cause.

That is why Jim wasn't able to escape from the clutches of alcoholism. He certainly tried, but in all of his attempts, he merely tried to deal with and control the *symptom*. As long as he felt in control, everything seemed okay. Then, as soon as a circumstance arose that showed him he wasn't in control, he escaped and resorted back to alcohol.

Eventually I had the opportunity to go back to Jim and talk to him about the significance of his statement, "Help me...I'm out of control." Today, Jim knows and recognizes his misplaced dependency and is in the process of learning to live by faith, moment by moment.

## How Satan Gains Control

Before we go further, I think it is important for us to understand some specifics about control. I do not mean to say that we are puppets and Satan can manipulate us in any way he chooses. Remember, whatever or whomever we depend upon will ultimately control us. We fall under Satan's control when we believe his lies rather than trust God's truth.

When we refuse to be controlled by our Creator, we have no choice except to be controlled by some other influence. When you and I were born again of the Spirit of God, we were born again spiritually. The Holy Spirit took up residence in our lives. So we who are Christians are indwelled by the Holy Spirit of God—Jesus lives in us. But this new spiritual creation that we have become is still housed in a temporal body of flesh. Temporal, but real. Within that body of flesh resides indwelling sin.

In the Garden, the temptation to be like God came from a source outside Adam and Eve. When they believed Satan's lie, that desire to be like God became a part of them. This indwelling sin has since been passed on from generation to generation. It is a part of every one of us from the moment we enter this world. We will not escape the desires of the flesh until God releases us from our earthly bodies to be with Him.

And what is indwelling sin? The same as original sin—the desire to control. Indwelling sin is the propensity to *want* to control our circumstances and everyone around us that has anything to do with our circumstances. So what do we see in the world around us?

The President tries to control Congress. Congress works to control the President. Husbands try to control their wives, and wives try to control their husbands. (Or, husbands try to control the television remote while wives try to control the thermostat.) Children try to manipulate and control their parents, and parents try to control their kids. Pastors try to control their congregation, and congregations try to control their pastors.

Now this may sound harsh, but we are nothing but a bunch of control freaks!

Indwelling sin wants us to believe the lie that we *can* be or *should* be in control. The flesh wants to have everything done according to its will—immediately, if possible. It wants to control the way people treat us. It wants to control our circumstances. It wants to control our destiny. Under Satan's lie, the flesh in its pride thinks it is able to run things.

Because of our conscious or unconscious desire for control, we think things would be better if only we were in charge: *If only I were president of the United States. If only I could run the church. If only I was in charge of the company. If only I could just get my wife to shape up. If only I could get my husband to do the things on my to-do list.*

How does Satan control our minds? By convincing us that we could be happier if we were in control of our circumstances. When we believe this, we lead a life of frustration and stress. We walk through life thinking we are in control when, in reality, we are under Satan's control and his lies are directing the course of our lives.

## Control Mechanisms

As long as you continue trying to control the circumstances of your life, you will respond to adverse circumstances in fear and anger and employ control mechanisms to protect yourself from further disappointment. We can categorize our control mechanisms into three areas: *exhibitionism, clinging,* and *attack.*

Think about this for a moment. If you walked up and hit me in the face by accident, the next time you walked by I would have my fists up just to make sure you didn't hit me in the face again. Our emotions work the same way. If you hurt me emotionally just once, the next time I am going to have some control mechanism in place to make sure you don't hurt me again.

We can see these kinds of control mechanisms on display in children. They may use temper tantrums and crying to get their own way. As adults, however, our attempts to control are more sophisticated. We may use withdrawal, silent treatments, pouting, putting people on guilt trips, or vengeance. Why do we do this? It's because our flesh wants to be satisfied. My flesh demands that you love me by doing what I want you to do. When you don't cooperate, and I'm depending upon you to fulfill the desires of my flesh, I will set up control mechanisms to try and ensure that you begin doing what I want you to do.

One such mechanism is **exhibitionism**. This includes reckless living, sexual promiscuity, profanity, gambling and so on. One approach to drawing attention to ourselves through exhibitionism is by *showing off.* We mostly see this in young children—they show off to get attention and acceptance. But adults do this too.

Another way we attempt to take control is through a *temper tantrum*. This communicates, "I want my way, and I want it now!"

*Withdrawal* is is often used as an effective control tool. The silent treatment. You want your mate to respond in a certain way and she doesn't. So you sit and hide behind the newspaper. There is no communication. Does this sound childish? Children cry and pout for effect, which is a ploy to get their own way.

Some people go to even further extremes, exhibiting *bizarre behavior*. We've seen this many times. In the sixties and seventies, America had its hippie revolution. More recently we've seen bizarre hairstyles and dress among our young. What are these kids saying? They are crying out, "I want to be noticed and satisfied in a certain way. So if long hair, or a rainbow mohawk, or shabby clothes, or a ring in my nose will get me noticed and get people doing what I want them to do for me, then that's what I will do."

Another control mechanism is ***clinging***. We see this in people who try to buy friendships. Clingers can't stand not being around others, so they "buy" friendships by giving the impression of being extremely helpful. Perhaps you know of an employee who absolutely can't stand not being noticed by the boss. He or she will work day and night to ensure his approval. Or what about a family where one member is constantly seeking approval by doing nice things for other family members? Or a wealthy person who uses his money to buy compliance from his children? People who cling to others cannot stand any sort of disapproval, so they try in every way to win other people's affections.

I know a family in Dallas in which the grown children refuse to give in to monetary bribery. Their mother is constantly giving them money, but the kids refuse to accept it and comply with her requests because of the strings attached to the "gift." So she periodically attempts to place them under guilt to force compliance. If she can't force her family to do her bidding any other way, she will get sick so that they will have to take care of her.

A third control mechanism is **attack**—lashing out at those whom we are afraid of losing. For example, let's say someone doesn't like you, so you start calling him or her names or put that person on a guilt trip. You're saying, "I'll teach you not to like me." You'll show this person that rejection doesn't pay. You'll try to shame him or her into loving you.

The attack mode often imposes either physical or mental punishment. Often the mental punishment has far worse consequences with regard to interpersonal relationships. People do not forget easily how someone treats them. When you shame someone into loving you, that person will love you out of guilt and eventually will resent what you have done to him or her. In the end, instead of being drawn closer to you, he or she is repelled farther away.

Note that all of these control mechanisms are designed to accomplish one purpose: *to control others to get one's own way.*

Unfortunately, they don't work! Whenever we try to control our circumstances through exhibitionism, clinging, or attack, we fall under the control of Satan's lie that we can be like God.

## The Success That Leads to Nowhere

Life offers many examples of people who, when observed from the outside, looked as if they were in total control. But as we have learned, no one is ever in control (or out of control). Even though their lives may look like the picture of success, there is something more important than appearance.

For example, consider where nine of the most successful men in the world found themselves 25 years after they had gathered in 1923 for a very important meeting that took place at the Edgewater Beach Hotel in Chicago.

The president of the largest independent steel company, Charles Schwab, died in bankruptcy and lived on borrowed money for the last five years of his life. The president of the greatest utility company, Samuel Insull, died a fugitive from justice and penniless in a foreign land. The president of the largest gas company, Howard Hopson, lost his sanity. The greatest wheat speculator, Arthur Cotton, died abroad insolvent. The president of the New York Stock Exchange, Richard Whitney, was released from Sing Sing Penitentiary. Albert Fall, a member of the president's cabinet, was pardoned so he could die at home. The greatest "bear" on Wall Street, Jesse Livermore, had committed suicide. The head of the greatest monopoly, Ivar Krueger, also had died at his own hands, as had the president of the Bank of International Settlements, Leon Fraser.

All of these men had chosen to learn the art of making a living, but none of them chose to learn *how to live!*

Another one of the wealthiest men in the world was Howard Hughes. He enjoyed a lifestyle many of us could only imagine. He had good looks, charm, and money to buy anything he wanted. He set the standard for the lifestyles of the rich and famous. And yet, he died in total obscurity, living like a hermit in a state of insanity. Even after his death, he remains an enigma. Reporters are still trying to put together the pieces of his shattered life. How did he go so far astray?

More recently the world was captivated by the gregarious smile and enormous talent of Magic Johnson. His "magical" skills on the basketball court have placed him among the game's all-time greats. His duels with Larry Bird during the Lakers-Celtics championship series in the

1980s comprise some of the most memorable moments in basketball history. To everyone looking on, Magic was a man on top of the world. He had everything—championship rings, money, cars, a beautiful wife and family. He was looked up to as a role model by many of his peers as well as by a multitude of young people across the nation. What a shock it was to hear him announce that he had contracted the HIV virus and was retiring from the game. What went wrong?

Hollywood has produced numerous examples of people who seemed to be in control. But, whether we're talking about the athlete O.J. Simpson or the actress Marilyn Monroe, the same story goes on and on. The world admires them for their so-called achievements, not realizing that there is something more important than outward success.

All of these people seemed to be in control of their destiny, but in every case it eventually became obvious that they were not in control at all. The choice to pursue the things of this world, which seemed to them an assurance of success, instead led them down a path of sorrow and pain. We too are confronted with the same choice: Do we choose to depend upon the One who created and loves us, or do we put our lives under the control of the one who deceives?

When you took high school chemistry, you learned that in order to make an experiment work you had to have a constant. Every variable must, in some way, be connected to a constant. The same is true in our lives. Without a constant, we cannot make this experiment of life work. There is nothing constant about us. We are nothing but a walking variable. This is why it is necessary for us to recognize our need for a constant in life—and the only constant in this world is Christ and His Word.

# 7
## Where Do We Go for Answers?

We have learned that feelings are by-products of our thoughts. Feelings in themselves are neither good nor bad. They cannot discern between fact or fiction. That's why it's so important for us to guard what we think because our minds are being continually bombarded with all kinds of thoughts every moment of the day.

In this chapter, we will see that God's Word is true, and what He says can lead us to think properly. For some Christians, this chapter will be a welcomed relief when they become aware of their thinking patterns. However, it will be a challenge for those who have compromised their thinking by combining psychological thought with biblical truth.

I am convinced that when Christians blend psychological thought with biblical truth, they deny the admonishment of the Bible to seek not "the counsel of the ungodly" (Psalm 1:1 KJV). This blending of psychology with the Word of God creates what I call "chocolate-milk Christianity." When you blend pure chocolate with pure milk, you lose the purity of both.

Jesus said in Matthew 9:17 that you cannot put new wine into old wineskins. When wine ferments or ages, it expands the skins to their ultimate capacity. The problem with pouring new wine into older, already-expanded skins is that the skins are not able to keep expanding. Rather, they burst, and you end up losing both the skins and the wine.

Although Jesus gave this illustration to talk about the Old and New Covenants, the principle applies in regard to psychological thought and Christian truth. You cannot pour man's wisdom into God's truth and expect to get anything but a watered-down mixture of the two. With this blend you can't discern between what is true and what is error, and you have nothing solid to stand on when the trials and tribulations of life come your way.

---

*You cannot pour
man's wisdom into God's truth
and expect to get anything but a
watered-down mixture of the two.*

---

You may find it surprising to know that I first learned about keeping the truth of the Gospel pure from a Christian psychologist named Henry Brandt—shortly after I became a Christian. Dr. Brandt was an unusual psychologist because he did not rely on his psychological training to counsel people. He knew that if he was going to help people, he would have to depend on something more solid than human philosophy. He stood on the inerrancy of God's Word and the total sufficiency of Jesus Christ to meet every need of the human heart. Unfortunately, today in Christian circles, he is a rare breed.

I greatly admire Dr. Brandt because in the 25 years I have known him, he has never wavered on his stance regarding the Bible. To this day he is still pointing people to Christ. Under his influence, I learned the importance of standing solidly on the Word of God. He helped me to see that if I want to know the answers to life, the Bible is the only place to go.

To have a solid foundation, we must build our lives on Christ and His Word. Jesus illustrated this in the Sermon on the Mount when He said:

> Therefore everyone who hears these words of mine and puts them into practice is like a wise man who built his house on the rock. The rain came down, the streams rose, and the winds blew and beat against that house; yet it did not fall, because it had its foundation on the rock. But everyone who hears these words of mine and does not put them into practice is like a foolish man who built his house on sand. The rain came down, the streams rose, and the winds blew and beat against that house, and it fell with a great crash (Matthew 7:24-27).

In those verses you will notice that the storm hit *both* the house built on the rock as well as the house built on sand. Having our foundation on the rock does not eliminate trials and tribulations. However, putting Christ's words into practice enables us to stand through the storms of life and live above our circumstances.

But, how can we know for sure that Christ's Word is reliable and that He holds the answers to all of life's situations? Let's examine the claims of Jesus Christ to see why we can have total confidence in the truth of the Bible.

## Who Do You Say I Am?

Several years ago, on a cross-country flight, I talked with a man sitting next to me. We talked superficially at first, but eventually our conversation turned to Christianity.

I asked Mike, "Has anyone ever shared with you what it means to know Jesus Christ in a personal way?"

Mike began to fidget and pull nervously at his tie. While many people are willing to discuss religion or God, they become noticeably uncomfortable when you mention the name of Jesus Christ.

Mike's reply to my simple and straightforward question was, "Do you really believe that story about Noah and the ark?"

I thought, *Where did that come from? I thought I was talking about a personal relationship with Jesus Christ. How did Noah enter the picture?*

His question wasn't unusual. I have shared Christ with many people who have asked the same question or similar ones, such as, "Was Jonah really swallowed by a whale?" or, "Did the Red Sea really split for Moses?" People use these questions as smoke screens. What they are really saying is, "I don't believe that the Bible is true, so don't bother me with that Jesus stuff."

I responded to Mike's question with another question: "Who do you think Jesus Christ is?"

With somewhat of a surprised look, he said, "What does that have to do with Noah and the ark?"

"Everything," I answered. "You see, the real issue in deciding whether or not we can trust the validity of the Bible is determined by our answer to the question, 'Who is Jesus Christ?'"

"He claimed to be God, and if He *is* God and He said there *was* an ark, then there was an ark. If He isn't God, then who cares? If Jesus is God and God said that we were created by God, then that ends the argument of evolution. On the other hand, if He is not God, who cares where we came from? Yet we are still stuck with these questions: Who am I? Why am I here? And where am I going?"

I then asked Mike, "Could I share with you why I have come to the conviction that Jesus is who He said He is—

God?" He was open to that, and we spent the rest of the trip exploring not the justification for Noah being in an ark, but the clear evidence of the deity of Christ.

Mike did not make an open acceptance of Christ that day, but the seed of truth was planted in his mind and the responsibility for it to grow is now in God's hands.

In order for us to accept the Bible as the Word of God, then, we must first answer Christ's question to His disciples: "Who do you say I am?" (Matthew 16:15).

## Christ's Claims About Himself

Throughout history, man has responded to Jesus' question in various ways. Some have said that He was a great moral teacher. Others have acknowledged Him as a great religious leader. Still others have called Him a great revolutionary. These responses show a high regard for Jesus, but they fail to come to grips with the issue of who He claimed to be.

Concerning Christ's claims, C.S. Lewis wrote this in his book *Mere Christianity:*

> A man who was merely a man and said the sort of things Jesus said would not be a great moral teacher. He would either be a lunatic—on a level with the man who says he is a poached egg—or else he would be the Devil of Hell. You must make your choice. Either this man was, and is, the Son of God: or else a madman or something worse. You can shut Him up for a fool; you can spit at Him and kill Him as a demon; or you can fall at His feet and call Him Lord and God. But let us not come with any patronizing nonsense about His being a great human teacher. He has not left that open to us. He did not intend to.

As Lewis said, Christ's claims were so outrageous that they leave us with only three options: Jesus was either a liar, or a lunatic, or He was telling the truth when He said that He is the Son of the living God. Let's consider, what Jesus said about Himself.

## Equality with God

In John 5:15, Christ healed an invalid. The Pharisees objected to this on the grounds that the miracle occurred on the Sabbath, violating their traditions. Jesus' response was, "My Father is always at His work to this very day, and I, too, am working" (John 5:17). The Jews knew what Christ was claiming and were outraged: "For this reason the Jews tried all the harder to kill Him; not only was He breaking the Sabbath, but He was even calling God His own Father, making *Himself equal with God*" (John 5:18, emphasis added).

## The Promised Messiah

In another intense encounter with the Pharisees, Christ again made statements about Himself that no ordinary human would dare to make:

> "Your father Abraham rejoiced at the thought of seeing my day; he saw it and was glad." "You are not yet fifty years old," the Jews said to Him, "and you have seen Abraham!" "I tell you the truth," Jesus answered, "before Abraham was born, I am!" At this, they picked up stones to stone Him, but Jesus hid Himself, slipping away from the temple grounds (John 8:56-59).

Abraham lived about 2,000 years before this incident, yet Jesus asserted, "Before Abraham was born, I am!" He claimed to have existed before Abraham, and His words, "I am" had special significance. When Moses spoke with God in the burning bush, he asked, "Suppose I go to the Israelites and say to them, 'The God of your fathers has sent me to you,' and they ask me, 'What is His name?'

Then what shall I tell them?" (Exodus 3:13). God answered, "I am who I am. This is what you are to say to the Israelites: 'I AM has sent me to you'" (Exodus 3:14). So when Christ said, "Before Abraham was born, *I am!*" He was claiming to be the One who spoke with Moses from the burning bush! It is no wonder the Pharisees picked up stones to stone Him!

Imagine the reaction I would receive from listeners if I went on the radio one night and said, "Folks, I've been teaching you for a long time, but I forgot to tell you something: I'm God." I don't think I would be able to finish the program before the fellows with the butterfly nets and straitjackets came to take me away!

---

*Jesus did not claim to merely **know** the answers to the problems we face in life; He claimed to be **the** answer.*

---

For me to claim to be God would be an absolutely ridiculous statement because I would not be able to back up my claim. But when Christ claimed Himself to be God, there was nothing inconsistent about His claims and the life that He lived here on earth. I believe people often miss the full impact of what Christ claimed about Himself because, coming from Him, these statements seem perfectly logical.

### The Answer to Our Heart Problems

Jesus amplified His claim to be God through what are known as the seven great "I ams." In these statements, Jesus did not claim to merely *know* the answers to the problems we face in life; He claimed to be *the* answer. That is why Christ always pointed people to Himself. *"Come to Me,* all you who are weary and burdened, and *I* will give you rest" (Matthew 11:28, emphasis added). In the gospel of John, He said, "I am the bread of life" (6:35), "I am the light of the world" (8:12), "I am the gate" (10:9), "I am the good shepherd" (10:11), "I am the resurrection and the life" (11:25), "I am the way and the truth and the life" (14:6), and, "I am the vine; you are the branches. If a man remains in Me and I in him, he will bear much fruit; apart from Me you can do nothing" (15:5).

Attached to each claim is a promise to fulfill the deepest needs and desires of the human heart. We were created in such a way that only God can fulfill them. When we come to Christ realizing that He is God and that only He can meet our needs, our search comes to an end. Like Jesus said to the woman at the well, "Whoever drinks the water I give him will never thirst" (John 4:14).

Also, John 5:39-40 tells us, "You diligently study the Scriptures because you think that by them you possess eternal life. These are the Scriptures that testify about Me, yet you refuse to come to Me to have life." This is why our source and foundation for life must be Christ and His Word.

Have you ever studied a book to know its author? I find it interesting that in all my years of attending school, I never studied a book to get to know the author. Rather, I and my fellow students studied books to learn their contents. We tried to learn and understand what the author wrote, but we never investigated the author. Unfortunately, this is the same approach many of us use when we study the Bible. We study the Book to get to know what is in the Book, and in so doing miss the author. The fact is, the Bible is the only book we read for the sole purpose of getting to know the author. This is why in John 17:17 Jesus said, *"Your* word is truth." It is the Word of God that points us to Jesus, who claimed to be the truth. That being the case, the validity of the Bible rests totally on the person of Jesus Christ.

What is the significance of all that? Simply this: If Jesus is God and He said that His Word is truth, then we can learn to live in dependency upon God's Word with full confidence not only in its truth but its ability to set us free. "So if the Son sets you free, you will be free indeed" (John 8:36).

## A Portrait of Change

One of the most powerful living demonstrations of this truth is Chris. I met Chris when I was teaching at Mt. Hermon Conference Center near Santa Cruz, California. He was dying from AIDS, which he had contracted through a promiscuous, homosexual lifestyle. He had given up his old life in exchange for a vibrant relationship with Jesus Christ, and had joined forces with his brother to share with others the truths that set him free from bondage.

How did Chris's life change so dramatically? How was he able to live so victoriously despite his circumstances? I asked him to tell me a little about his background.

"I came from an upper middle-class family in New Mexico," he said. He explained that his parents were Christians, but their lives were controlled by bitterness and legalism. "As a child and adolescent I was very quiet and withdrawn. As things progressed in my life I came to the conclusion that I was a homosexual. What was communicated to me on Sundays from the pulpit made me think that I was going straight to hell. I was never taught that my identity was that of a child of God, saved by grace and totally accepted by Him."

Chris's parents found out about his homosexuality when he was 15. They sent him to a professional therapist. Chris wasn't interested in receiving help at the time, so he merely said what he thought the counselor wanted to hear and made him think he was cured.

"But secretly in my mind I was already burning in hell for something I believed I was born with," he said. "And the only relief I could find for this constant fear of the fire of hell was a bottle of alcohol and all the drugs I could get my hands on."

Chris lived this destructive lifestyle for many years, going from one experience to another, desperately trying to find something to fill the emptiness in his soul.

"I knew something had to change," Chris continued. "I thought maybe I should go back to the therapist. But coming out of the counseling sessions, I still felt empty."

Chris's life degenerated further. He became a male prostitute, pierced his body because he "enjoyed the pain," and finally tried to end his life and was committed to a mental hospital.

When he was released, he determined that the way to change his life was to eliminate his addiction. But his resolve lasted only two days. He then enrolled in a 12-step program. While it didn't solve his problems, it did turn his thoughts towards God, and his thinking about God was challenged. Then, he was reunited with his brother in Arizona and was amazed at the changes he saw in him. Chris eventually visited the same counselor his brother had seen.

"I realized that this counseling was different," Chris told me. "I had made a provision with the counselor that my sexuality was not going to be a topic for discussion. He agreed to it. The counselor's purpose was to help me become free mentally and emotionally.

"During the course of the counseling something in me was changing. I was becoming free of the bitterness that had driven me all my life. I had become a slave to rejection for which I set myself up in most cases. Eventually, I remembered that as a child I had accepted Christ but had not understood that my sins were forgiven and that He had given me His life."

The counselor had recommended that Chris read my book *Classic Christianity*. As he read, he became convinced that God loved and accepted him unconditionally. He wept as he said, "At that point I truly realized that I was not a homosexual or any of the names I had been called in life. Instead, I was a child of the living God. In the sight of God, through the blood of Jesus Christ, I had been made perfect. The peace, love, and joy that I experienced at that realization was indescribable. I knew at that point that God had a perfect plan for my life. It was not a duty for me to live for Him. It became a *joy!*"

Sometime later, Chris wrote to me, "I never dreamed this would be possible. I no longer engage in homosexual activity, not because I can't...but why would I want to? I have found Christ to be the answer to all my problems. I have found in Him the love and acceptance that I was always searching for in people. Praise be to God, He truly does love me! Now I am able to live the kind of life I have always wanted."

There wasn't much I could write back to Chris except to praise God with him for His incredible love. You see, that counselor and I can't take credit for the change in Chris's life. All we did was proclaim the truth that is available to everyone. It was the truth of God's Word that renewed Chris's mind and changed his life. He couldn't change his circumstances, but he could change his thinking, and when he did, he achieved victory over his circumstances!

The same power demonstrated in Chris's life is available to you and me, but the choice is ours. We can believe what the world says about us, or we can choose to believe God. If you choose to begin the process of allowing God to renew your mind, you will soon find out the truth about who you really are. And that is what we want to turn our attention to now.

# 8
## *Renewing Your Mind*

There is only one source of truth—Jesus Christ. Unfortunately, we live in a world that is "under the control of the evil one" (1 John 5:19). As such, our minds are constantly receiving input from either Satan and the world or from God and His Word. If we do not rely constantly on God's Word as our source of input, it can become difficult for us to determine if what we are thinking and feeling is based on truth, fact, fantasizing, or a lie.

## The World's Programming

The world, with its deceptive ideas and thinking, gains access to our minds through our five senses—primarily through the eye and ear gate. Now when I talk about the world, I am not talking about the physical world in which we live; I am referring to any human understanding, philosophy, or mind-set that does not have its origins in God. 1 John 2:15-16 describes the world like this:

> Do not love the world or anything in the world. If anyone loves the world, the love of the Father is not in him. For everything in the world—the cravings of sinful man, the lust of his eyes and the

> boasting of what he has and does—comes not
> from the Father but from the world.

Every day our minds are constantly bombarded with sights and sounds that appeal to our cravings, the lust of our eyes, and the boasting of what we have and do. These temptations produce desires and feelings which we can act out. The pattern, then, is this: think it, feel it, and then do it. That is how we naturally live when we are not applying God's truth to our lives.

Notice that when we listen to the world's programming, our actions follow our feelings. But, God never intended us to be slaves to our fickle emotions. That is why the Bible tells us not to conform to the patterns of this world. We live *in* the world, but we are told not to be *of* the world. This is like saying to a ship that you are to be in the ocean but not of the ocean. If you've ever traveled by ship, you know what I mean. You do not have to be a nuclear scientist to figure out that you had better not be of the ocean because the minute that you are, you will sink.

## God's Programming

With God's programming, there is a totally different pattern. First, God puts His truth in our minds and hearts through His Word, and renews our thinking and attitudes through His Spirit, who lives in us if we are born again. Then we are to respond to that truth with an attitude of faith—that is, trust that what God says is true and then act it out. This results in godly emotions. The correct order is thoughts first, then faith in God's Word (which produces actions), and then feelings.

For example, Scripture tells us to be anxious for nothing. Is anxiety an emotion? Definitely. But is it a desirable emotion? Most people would agree it is not. So what do we want to replace it with? Don't we prefer peace? Most of us long for never-ending internal peace, but the world can't provide that for us. However, Scripture shows us how to find it: "Do not be anxious about anything, but in everything, by prayer and petition, with thanksgiving, present your requests to God" (Philippians 4:6). What happens when you do that? "The peace of God, which transcends all understanding, will guard your hearts and your minds in Christ Jesus" (Philippians 4:7).

Let's think about that for a moment. Imagine a situation that makes you feel anxious. Maybe you have tried several times to reach your elderly parents on the phone and no one answers, and you are wondering if they are all right. Perhaps your child has a doctor's appointment and you are worried about the findings of the tests that will be done. Maybe your spouse is traveling and you're concerned because the weather is bad. I'm sure you can think of many other situations that would create anxiety.

Let's say that in that moment of anxiety, God's Word enters your mind and says, "Don't be anxious."

You answer, "Okay, Lord. I don't want to be anxious. What should I do?"

God answers, "I'll tell you what to do. I want you to pray and, with thanksgiving, make your request known unto Me."

Now you face a choice. You can continue stewing in your anxiety. Or you can act by faith and do what God says, regardless of how you feel. It's as if God is saying, "I know your problem, and I also know the solution. You have no reason to be anxious. Instead, trust Me and give Me your request."

Now what is God's promise? It is *not* that you will receive exactly what you request. Rather, you will receive the "peace of God which transcends all understanding." Is peace an emotion? Definitely. Jesus said, "Peace I leave with you; my peace I give you. I do not give to you as the world gives. Do not let your hearts be troubled and do not be afraid" (John 14:27). In other words, God gives a different kind of peace—one that comes from knowing His faithfulness to you.

So there are your two options. You can deal with the flesh through the mind, which feeds the emotions and leads to your physical actions. Or you can let the Spirit feed your mind, which leads you to act by faith (physical) and results in godly emotions.

## Contrasting Worldviews

By way of example, if your goal is to seek success at any price and make as much money as you can, your emotional state will depend on how you are doing in your endeavor at any given time. Yet some of the most unhappy and unfulfilled people are the ones we think of as successful and rich. Success, from God's perspective, is this: "Seek first His kingdom and His righteousness, and all these things will be given to you as well" (Matthew 6:33), and "Do not store up for yourselves treasures on earth, where moth and rust destroy, and where thieves break in and steal. But store up for yourselves treasures in heaven, where moth and rust do not destroy, and where thieves do not break in and steal" (Matthew 6:19-20).

You see, human philosophy concentrates on how well we do and how much we accomplish in this world. The world says push ahead and promote yourself for if you don't, someone else will get there first. Excel at any cost. Be somebody. Do whatever it takes to succeed. If you don't look after yourself, no one else will. After all, God helps those who help themselves. Did you know that this saying is *not* in the Bible?

In contrast, God tells us that we are here for just a brief period of time. Our destiny is eternity. God is eternal, and He wants us to concentrate on what is eternal, not temporal. He wants us to humble ourselves and serve others. Philippians 2:3 tells us, "Do nothing out of selfish ambition or vain conceit, but in humility consider others better than yourselves." What a contrast to what the world says!

Adopting the world's way of thinking is a sure way to lack a sense of fulfillment in life. For example, many single people think they will never know happiness until they get married. Then there are married people who think they cannot be happy unless they're single. Both groups think that the way to happiness is to change their status.

Or, how about this one? Many people think that if they could just move to another location, then they would be happy. The only problem with that is when you move to another location, *you* go there too!

When Amy and I visited Hawaii some time ago, I was amazed at how many people appeared to be grumpy even in that earthly paradise. How in the world can anyone be unhappy in Hawaii? I will admit that it may seem better to be miserable on Waikiki Beach than in Dallas, but the simple fact is that if you are unhappy in one place, most likely, you will be unhappy in another.

Only when you begin to trust the Lord and rely on His love and grace will you learn to be content regardless of where you live or how bad your circumstances seem. That's why the apostle Paul, when he was imprisoned in Rome, was able to write, "I have learned to be content whatever the circumstances" (Philippians 4:11).

Here are some more contrasts:

The world says, "Be pretty and sexy." God says, "Don't concentrate on external adornment but rather on developing the inner qualities of a gentle and quiet spirit."

The world says, "Take revenge, and make sure you don't get hurt again." God says, "Revenge belongs to Me."

The world says, "If it feels good, do it." Jesus said, "Not My will, but Yours be done."

The world says, "Everything is relative." God says, "Jesus is the truth and His Word is truth."

It is clear, then, that the world's philosophies and God are totally opposed to one another. That's why modern psychology doesn't have the answers to man's problems. The answers we get from psychologists may seem to make sense, but it's important to examine the root beliefs of psychology. Only then can we discern that psychology falls far short of what the Bible has to offer.

## Differences Between Psychology and the Bible

The chart on the following page shows the stark contrast between the general premises of modern psychology and the Word of God in regard to some basic issues.

As we look at this chart, it is evident that Jesus spoke as one having authority on the subject of man and the basic issues of life. The problem with most people, however, is that when it comes to the truth, they would rather not be quite so dogmatic. They think it is reasonable to accept what the psychological world says to be true. After all, the world says, "All truth is God's truth." But as we've seen above, in our attempt to harmonize the differences, we are left asking, "What is truth?"

## Discerning That Which Is True

The apostle Paul warned us about this kind of humanistic thinking: "See to it that no one takes you captive through hollow and deceptive philosophy, which depends on human tradition and the basic principles of this world rather than on Christ" (Colossians 2:8). Whenever we open ourselves to the philosophies of this world and lean on our own understanding, we will be taken captive by them.

| Issue | Modern Psychology | Word of God |
|---|---|---|
| • God | • God is dead or at best irrelevant. | • "The fool says in his heart, 'There is no God'" (Psalm 53:1). |
| • Man | • Man is an evolving animal. | • Man was created in the image of God (1 Corinthians 11:7; James 3:9). |
| • Truth | • There is no truth; everything is relative. | • "Grace and truth came through Jesus Christ" (John 1:17).<br>• Jesus said, "Your word is truth" and "If you hold to My teaching. . . . you will know the truth" (John 17:17; 8:31). |
| • Meaning of Sin | • If man behaves wrongly, it is because he is "sick" and needs therapy.<br>• It is only wrong if you think it is wrong. Man is not sinful; just give him a little time and everything will be okay. | • Man's effort to find true meaning to life is impossible apart from total dependency upon God.<br>• Man is sinful and needs a new heart: "You must be born again" (John 3:7).<br>• "He will convict the world of . . . sin, because men do not believe in Me" (John 16:8-9). |
| • Purpose | • Eat, drink and be merry, for tomorrow we die. | • Jesus said, "This is eternal life: that they may know You, the only true God, and Jesus Christ whom You have sent" (John 17:3). |

I am constantly amazed at how Christians do not stop and think this through. In John 14:6, Jesus claimed to be *the way, the truth, and the life.* If any evangelical Christian were to claim that there are many ways to God, we would label him a heretic. If another Christian said eternal life could be found outside of Jesus, we would label him a heretic as well. Yet, when it comes to truth, we are open and readily accept most anything that comes our way that sounds like truth. We must be careful that we don't use "the way" and "the life" as Christian bookends to hold up a mixture of worldly philosophies combined with some truth of God.

When Jesus said, "I *am* the truth," He was affirming that He is the only truth. He's the author and originator of truth. Everything that comes our way must be filtered through His truth, which is the Word of God. Therefore, to experience freedom, we must not let "the way" and "the life" merely be bookends. We must accept the fact that Jesus *is* the truth as well. He is the foundation upon whom we should build our lives and the compass who should direct our paths.

---

*The Word of God —
our spiritual compass.*

---

In my conferences, I often ask people to close their eyes for a moment and point their finger north. Hands immediately go in all directions. Many people even point straight up, thinking that north is directly above them. There is always laughter when they open their eyes and see all the different directions hands are pointing. Then I pull out a compass and show them true north. Why do I conduct this experiment? To show that we cannot determine accurately where north is apart from a compass. We need something more reliable than our internal sense of direction. The same is true in regard to spiritual matters. If we are going to know what truth is, we must have something more reliable than our feelings, and that is the Word of God—our spiritual compass.

In Matthew 7 we read that the storms in life are going to come regardless of our foundation. The only two choices we have are *which* foundation are we going to stand upon—the solid rock which is the Word of God, or the worldly influences that come from Satan? It is only as we build our lives on Christ and His Word that we are prepared to live above the circumstances that come our way.

## Successful Preparation for Life's Crises

It began as a routine mission. In 70,000 flights over Bosnia, only two pilots had been shot down, neither of them Americans. Air Force Captain Scott O'Grady had no intention of being number three when he took off in his F-16 on June 2, 1995, to enforce the NATO no-fly zone. One moment he appeared to be in control. The next, his plane was rocked by a Soviet-made antiaircraft missile. Five miles above ground, he desperately grabbed for his ejection handle and pulled. His quick action saved him from a fiery death. But his ordeal had just begun.

After landing in enemy territory, Captain O'Grady scrambled for cover. For a moment, paralyzing fear gripped him—a natural response to his circumstances. Then he remembered his training. While he had never expected to be in such a predicament, he began to feel a strange sense of comfort because he knew he was prepared. His mind reviewed all the facts. He was in hostile territory and his job was to evade all enemies until help arrived. There was no time for wishful thinking. He had work to do.

Six days later, Captain O'Grady was rescued in dramatic fashion, capturing the imagination of a nation. He returned home to hero's welcome. But Captain O'Grady didn't consider himself a hero. He'd simply been in the wrong place at the wrong time. The key to his survival? Training. Captain Scott O'Grady never planned to be shot down, but he was prepared when it happened.

Like Captain O'Grady, we need to be prepared when the trials and tribulations of life hit us. Captain O'Grady was scared and frightened and could have relied on his instinct and feelings. Yet he was trained to handle the situation based on reliable and proven survival methods. Similarly, when the crises of life come our way, we need to turn to reliable truth rather than rely on our feelings and the philosophies of the world. If we depend on these, we will find that they are a hollow foundation and we will crumble under the pressures and stresses of life.

This is why it is so important that your foundation be built on Christ and His Word. It is God's Word that prepares us to live above the circumstances of life. Second Timothy 3:16-17 tells us, "All Scripture is God-breathed and is useful for teaching, rebuking, correcting and training in righteousness, so that the man of God may be thoroughly equipped for every good work." God's Word trains us and equips us to rely on the sufficiency of Christ. And it is in Him that we can truly experience an abundant life...and learn to live above our circumstances.

# 9
## *Discovering the Real You*

The joy of the Lord permeated Mark's attitude despite the constant pain that racked his body. Bracing himself on the shoulder of a friend, he slowly moved into a chair in front of the microphone. With his lovely young wife Linda beside him, they talked to the staff of *People to People* Ministries about the changes that had taken place in their lives since learning that his illness was terminal.

"When we learned that I was not going to regain my health," began Mark, "it was a real shock to us. We needed answers. With my church background, being a good Christian meant always *being* good. And I could never *be* good. The harder I tried to be good, the more I went out and did things I should not do."

Mark smiled as he thought back on his life.

"After a while, you just burn out. I mean, you try and try and try, and after a while you say, 'Well, I guess I can't do it. Maybe God will give me the benefit of the doubt for trying.'"

Then one day, like many other listeners, Mark was surfing the radio dial when he stumbled across the *People to People* radio broadcast while driving home from work. What he heard sounded radically different from what he had learned as a young Christian. He told his wife about the program and as they listened together, they began to find the answers they were so desperately looking for.

Mark continued, "It was a great relief to find out that Christ finished His work on the cross for us and that He no longer dealt with us on the issue of sin. A lot of burdens were lifted, as well as a lot of fear."

Mark's prognosis gave him many reasons to fear the future. He feared that his illness was "punishment for a rebellious and wretched lifestyle." This fear manifested a pointing finger that sneered: "You're paying for your sins, pal!" But as Mark continued to listen to the broadcast, he began to gain a whole new perspective as he recognized how God truly saw him and his situation.

Mark also arrived at a new perspective regarding his illness. He said, "I live now in total dependency upon Him. He is my life, and He is my sufficiency. He is the only One who keeps me from being so depressed that I would take my own life."

Linda nodded in agreement and added, "The Lord has brought so many loving and caring people into our lives who have been such a blessing to us. I know that I always have somebody out there who I can call who will listen to me and understand.

"We went through a period of time before finding *People to People* during which we said, 'It's not worth it.' When you're faced with losing the person whom you love most on this earth—if you don't know Christ—there seems to be no reason to go on. But the Lord touched both of our hearts and said, 'It's worth it. And you are worth it. You're important to Me. I will take care of you. I will never leave you nor forsake you.'"

Here was a young man in extreme pain as he struggled just to breathe. Yet he was able to say, "I'm ready to let go of my life and let God's will be done! What a wonderful feeling to be secure in Christ!"

I was humbled to learn that his last wish had been to attend one of our conferences just to say thank you for sharing the reality of Christ's love and grace. Two months later we received the news that Mark had finished his course and gone to be with the Lord. I wept because I missed my friend and grieved for his wife, yet I also rejoiced that he was no longer in pain and enjoying the presence of his Savior.

---

*Until we find our identity, we will be searching for the rest of our lives for peace and fulfillment.*

---

Over the next few months after Mark's death, I thought about the transformation that had taken place in his and Linda's lives. In the face of an overwhelmingly painful circumstance, how were they able to cope? What made the difference? What gave them the ability to rest so secure in God's love and grace?

As I contemplated the answers to those questions, I concluded that there was nothing mystical or mysterious. Clearly, Mark and Linda had become persuaded of their true identity in Christ. Understanding who they were in Christ changed how they looked at life and death in terms of their relationship with God and their circumstance.

### The Truth About Our Identity

One of the most important questions any person can ask is, "Who am I?" In this chapter, we are going to discuss the topic of identity and who, as Christians, we really are. The truths I am about to share about our identity are the same truths that enabled Mark and Linda to live above the most difficult circumstance of their young lives.

Discovering our true identity is a basic need of the human heart. Until we find our identity, we will be searching for the rest of our lives for peace and fulfillment. The issue is where are we going to go to find the answer. The options available are either Satan and the world, or Christ and His Word.

When we were little children, our identity was given to us by our parents. But as we grew, we came to want our own identity. So where did we turn? Some of us found our identity in our school, our peers, or our popularity with fellow students. And as adults, the most common place we find our identity is in our occupations. When you meet a person and ask what he or she does, invariably that person answers, "I'm a businessman," or "I'm a school teacher," or "I'm a doctor," or "I'm a lawyer," or "I'm a housewife," and so on. That person's identity is totally tied up in what he or she does.

Because of this false identity, many people suffer from severe depression, discouragement, apathy, and even die within a few years of retiring. Housewives, after their children have left home, feel that they are no longer needed and have lost their identity. These women are prime candidates for depression; the empty nest robs them of the feeling of being needed.

In today's world, there are all kinds of labels people use to identify themselves. Some people say, "I'm an alcoholic," or "I'm bulimic," or "I'm a manic depressive." The world seems anxious to put these labels on people, but where do you ever find these terms in the Bible? I've told many people that if you came up to Jesus and asked Him, "Who am I?" His answer would *not* be, "You are a paranoid schizophrenic," or a manic depressive or any other of those worldly labels.

Unfortunately, when it comes to identity, many Christians would rather listen to the world than to God. That's why in counseling, I try to help them identify their true selves.

Not long ago I had the opportunity to talk with a young man named Bruce. He said he needed help because he was an alcoholic. Rather than dealing with his drinking problem, I asked him about his relationship with Jesus Christ. I do this because if a person does not know Christ personally, then my counsel is going to sound foolish to him. A lost person cannot understand spiritual truth. The apostle Paul tells us that "the man without the Spirit does not accept the things that come from the Spirit of God, *for they are foolishness to him, and he cannot understand them,* because they are spiritually discerned" (1 Corinthians 2:14, emphasis added). Besides that, quite frankly, being lost is a much more severe problem than drinking too much.

Bruce told me about the day he placed his faith in Jesus Christ and became a child of the living God. He was genuine as he talked and was positive that Christ was in his heart.

In light of what we had just discussed, I asked him, "Bruce, are you an alcoholic, or are you a child of God?"

He thought for a moment, then answered, "Both, I guess."

"Bruce, think about it. You can't be both. You are either one or the other. If you see and identify yourself as an alcoholic, then drinking is merely an extension of who you are and is very natural to your identity. But, on the other hand, if you are a child of God, drinking is inconsistent with your identity as a child of God. You could be a child of God with a drinking problem, but the drinking does not cause or sustain your identity."

As we continued our conversation, Bruce began to realize his true identity in Christ and started to see that he was not an alcoholic but a child of God who was choosing an alternative dependency to help him cope with his daily problems. He was then able to let go of that old label and see himself only as God sees him. He realized that as a child of God, getting drunk didn't make sense anymore. It was through that realization that he was able to break free from his bondage to alcoholism.

Another way Christians identify themselves is by what denomination or church they belong to. Different people say, "I'm a Methodist," or "I'm a Lutheran," or "I'm an Episcopalian." But where do you find these identities in the Word of God? These labels have caused divisions among the body of Christ and have blinded us to what true Christianity is really about.

Satan doesn't care what label you adopt as long as it is not your true identity—a child of God. If Satan can convince you that you are something other than a child of God, he has derailed you into deception. With that in mind, let's take a look now at who we are and how God sees us. Let's meet *the real you.*

## Identifying the Real You

### You Are a Child of God

"To all who received Him, to those who believed in His name, He gave the right to become children of God" (John 1:12). Let me illustrate our new identity by comparing it to that of a jar. If there is nothing in a jar, its identity is precisely what it is: a jar. However, if you fill that jar with applesauce, it takes on a brand new identity—it is now a jar of applesauce. Not only has the jar changed in identity, but it has also changed in value. Its identity and value come from what is *in* the jar.

The same is true with our lives. We come into this world empty of God's Spirit. But when we receive Christ into our hearts as our Lord and Savior, He comes to take up residence in us and now we are children of God. Our new identity and value comes from who lives in us.

> You are . . . a son; and since you are a son, God
> has made you also an heir (Galatians 4:7).

One of the functions of the Holy Spirit is to continually remind us of this truth. Romans 8:15-16 says, "You did not receive a spirit that makes you a slave again to fear, but you received the Spirit of sonship. And by him we cry, 'Abba, Father.' The Spirit Himself testifies with our spirit that we are God's children."

When trouble comes, we sometimes question God's love and start to doubt our salvation. And Satan is right there to help us along the way, saying, "How could you be a Christian with all this bad stuff happening to you?" Then you may start questioning the sincerity of your faith and wonder, "Maybe I didn't really mean what I was praying when I received Christ." This kind of thinking may convince you that you aren't even saved! Of course when such negative thoughts go through your head, God seems a million miles away. Even though the Lord has promised that He will never leave us nor forsake us (Hebrews 13:5), our emotions tell us a different story.

During these times of doubt, our deepest need is to know that we belong to Him. That is why He placed His Spirit in our hearts—to bear witness with our spirits that we truly are children of God (Romans 8:16). It is the still, small voice of God's Spirit that will give you the encouragement, strength, and confidence to go through any circumstance knowing who you belong to and whom you can trust.

## You Are a Forgiven Person

While on the cross, Jesus prayed, "Father, forgive them, for they do not know what they are doing" (Luke 23:34). This forgiveness was extended to those who beat

Him, spat on Him, plucked His beard, cursed Him, stripped Him of His clothes, mocked Him, jammed a crown of thorns on His head, and nailed Him to a cross.

Often people say to me that they can't forgive themselves. I usually ask them this question: "Are your moral standards higher than those of God Himself?" Of course, these people are shocked, for they would never say such a thing. Yet, in essence, people who say they can't forgive themselves are saying, "God might have been able to forgive my sins, but I can't forgive them because my standards are higher than those of Jesus."

Such thinking is ludicrous. There isn't a sin that you could commit that wasn't covered by the blood of Christ and therefore forgiven. When someone asks, "Could Christ forgive me for _____(fill in the blank)?" The answer is that He already *has* forgiven you. You *are* a forgiven person.

Most Christians give lip service to this truth. The question is, do they really believe that *all* their sins have been forgiven? The best time to find out is during an adverse circumstance. When Mark was first diagnosed with a terminal illness, he thought God was punishing him for his past sins. Such thinking isn't unusual. The first question many of us ask when a trial comes our way is, "God, what have I done wrong? For what sin are you punishing me?"

But we should be careful about making a connection between trials and God's punishment. In the Scriptures, when Jesus encountered the man who was blind from birth, His disciples asked, "Rabbi, who sinned, this man or his parents, that he was born blind?" (John 9:2) The disciples thought that adverse circumstances were part of God's punishment of people's sins, and many Christians have that same perspective today. That's why we need our minds renewed. What was Christ's answer? John 9:3 tells us: "Neither this man nor his parents sinned...but this happened so that the work of God might be displayed in his life."

No, your adverse circumstances are not signs that God is punishing you for some of the sins you've committed. Trials and tribulations are part of life.

Because of Christ's death on the cross, God is no longer dealing with you on the basis of sin and death. The punishment for all your sins was placed upon the Lord Jesus Christ. Therefore, there is no more punishment left for you (Romans 8:1). Because of the cross, God is no longer counting your sins against you. He says in Hebrews 10:17, "Their sins and lawless acts, I will remember no more." God dealt with sin once and for all 2,000 years ago. Resting in the forgiveness that is yours is a key element of learning to live above your circumstances.

Contrary to what most of us think, then, God is not anxiously watching and thinking of new ways to punish us. He is satisfied with the work of Christ on our behalf. There is nothing left for Him to do in regard to sin. That is why the apostle Paul boldly proclaims, "He has rescued us from the dominion of darkness and brought us into the kingdom of the Son He loves, in whom we have *redemption, the forgiveness of sins*" (Colossians 1:13-14). If you are in Christ, you not only have redemption, you also have forgiveness of sins.

As wonderful as it is for God to forgive us, He did not stop there. As the Bible says, He became sin on our behalf so that we might become the righteousness of God in Him. "God made Him who had no sin to be sin for us, so that in Him we might become the righteousness of God" (2 Corinthians 5:21).

Before Christ could give you His righteousness, He had to cleanse you of all your unrighteousness.

Let me illustrate this point for you. Many years ago, a well-known razor blade company was planning to make a television commercial. In order to promote their new razor blades in a powerful demonstration, they sent out a representative to a homeless shelter to find two men who could work as models. The requirement was that they should have the thickest, most scruffy-looking beards imaginable. For their services the men would be paid $100 each. The representative found two men who filled the requirement. They were elated at the prospect of being on television and earning the money. They were told to be in front of the building at 8:00 A.M. sharp.

Wanting to look their best on national television, the two woke up early and decided to clean themselves up. When they arrived on location, the producer asked, "Where are the two men for the commercial?" They excitedly answered, "We are right here!" The producer screamed, "You shaved off your beards!" Surprised, the men looked at each other and explained how they wanted to look good on national television. The producer said, "We, too, wanted you to look good on TV, but only *after* we had cleaned you up. I'm sorry, but we can't use you!" These men, through their self-effort, blew their chance to make money and receive nationwide exposure.

So it is with many of us. We want to clean ourselves up to appear before God. But God wants to clean us up according to His purpose.

The Bible says that because of one man's sin (Adam), death reigned. But because of one man's life (Jesus), righteousness reigns (Romans 5:12-17). Many Christians have received the gift of forgiveness, but they fail to understand that they also have been given a gift of righteousness. It is that gift that gives us the assurance that we are totally acceptable in the sight of God and allows us to present our bodies to Christ as living sacrifices so that He can live His life through us.

You are now living as a new creation, clothed in the righteousness of Christ. Therefore, you and I stand in the presence of God wearing His righteousness, not our own.

You cannot perfect yourself or make yourself more pleasing to God. He has already accomplished everything for you in Jesus.

I call this transaction "the great exchange." You gave God everything you were—"dead in your sins and in the uncircumcision of your sinful nature" (Colossians 2:13). In turn, "God made you alive with Christ. He forgave us all our sins." In Him you have forgiveness, eternal life, righteousness, and acceptance. You used to be dead, but now you are alive—a brand new creation. The best way I can explain this "great exchange" is to have you envision yourself as a caterpillar. God created caterpillars with the capacity to become something entirely different. Through the process of metamorphosis, ugly caterpillars can be transformed into beautiful butterflies. Likewise, when you are born again, you become a new creation. You become holy and totally acceptable in His sight. You stand in Christ's life and His righteousness.

> It is because of him that you are in Christ Jesus, who has become for us wisdom from God—that is, our righteousness, holiness and redemption (1 Corinthians 1:30).

## You Are the Body of Christ

The apostle Paul tells us in 1 Corinthians 12:27, "Now you are the body of Christ, and each one of you is a part of it." How did we become a part of the body of Christ? We were placed into it the day we received Christ into our lives. The Bible says that we were all baptized by one Spirit into one body. Because of this truth we can say, "We belong to Christ and we belong to each other." We are a part of something bigger than ourselves.

Now don't misunderstand what I mean when I say we were *baptized* by one Spirit. Many people miss the meaning of this truth because they are thinking only of the act of baptism in water. First Corinthians 12:13, which says all of us were baptized by one Spirit into one body, is *not* talking about water baptism. It is talking about being placed into the body of Christ. No matter who you are, whether Jew or Greek, slave or free, we were all given the same Spirit (1 Corinthians 12:13). The gospel is equally available to all. Those who receive it become an important part of the body of Christ.

---

*We are part of an orchestra called the body of Christ. Our conductor is Jesus.*

---

God has arranged the parts of the body just as He wanted them to be—much like the conductor of an orchestra arranges each person according to what instrument he or she plays. When their efforts are combined, they produce a sound that is pleasing to the ears. Musically, they become united in accomplishing their goal. Even though each person is playing an individual instrument, they are all in perfect harmony.

We are part of an orchestra called the body of Christ. Our conductor is Jesus. When each part is walking in dependence on Jesus, we function as Christ intended us to, and together we can truly carry out His work in this world. If each part decides to do his or her own thing, we do not paint a very good picture of the love of Christ.

He is the head; we are the body. As the apostle Paul wrote, "Just as each of us has one body with many members, and these members do not all have the same function, so in Christ we who are many form one body, and each member belongs to all the others" (Romans 12:4-5).

## You Are Sealed in Christ.

In Ephesians 1:13 Paul tells us what happens at the moment of salvation: "You also were included in Christ when you heard the word of truth, the gospel of your salvation. Having believed, you were marked in Him with a seal, the promised Holy Spirit." When you are sealed, that means you are preserved. You cannot be snatched away from Christ. No one can take away your salvation, forgiveness, or righteousness. No one can remove you from the body of Christ to which you belong.

Let's go back to the jar I talked about earlier. A jar is cleansed before it is filled. Once it is cleansed, it is filled with applesauce (or some other ingredient), and then it is sealed. That seal protects and preserves the contents of the jar. Similarly, the Holy Spirit protects and preserves us until the day of redemption. He is the guarantee of the inheritance that is ours in Christ Jesus.

## You Are Free!

In Galatians 5:1, Paul wrote, "It is for freedom that Christ has set us free. Stand firm, then, and do not let yourselves be burdened again by a yoke of slavery."

Let's look back on those tragic days of slavery in our country. Imagine that you are at an auction where people are being sold as if they were cattle. There stands a big, strong man on the auction block. Because of his obvious strength, the bidding is competitive. The price climbs higher and higher, until finally a wealthy landowner acquires the slave for an extremely high price. The master approaches the slave, who is bound by chains around his legs and wrists, and demands the keys from the former owner. He bends down and unlocks the leg irons. Then he releases the chains on the slave's wrists. He looks the man in the eyes and says, "My son, go! You are free!"

The slave is stunned. "But you just bought me for a high price!" he cries.

"Yes, but I bought you to set you free."

Then the slave does an amazing thing. He asks the wealthy man, "Where do you live?"

"I live two miles down the road," is the answer.

"May I please go home with you?" asks the free man.

"You may. But not because you have to. Only if you want to. Not to be my slave, but to be my friend."

"Oh, but I want to," replies the free man. "Any man who would love me enough to buy me in order to set me free is the man I want to know and serve in love."

This story illustrates an important truth. You and I were slaves—slaves with sin as our master. But Christ paid the ransom to buy us out of that slave market. Under the grace of God, Jesus said, "I no longer call you servants, because a servant does not know his master's business. Instead, I have called you friends, for everything that I learned from my Father I have made known to you" (John 15:15). No longer do we have to listen to the dictates of the old master. We can be controlled by the same love and grace that motivated God to pay the price for us. So our response can be like that of the former slave—that of wanting to live with the one who set us free.

### You Are Totally Loved by God the Father

The apostle John wrote, "How great is the love the Father has lavished on us, that we should be called children of God! And that is what we are!" (1 John 3:1). Because of God's love, we have a brand new identity, and John tells us to remain or abide in that love: "As the Father has loved Me, so I have loved you. Now remain in my love" (John 15:9). It is as we abide and are convinced of the love of God that we are able to live above our circumstances.

The apostle Paul knew that he was totally loved by the Father. After he experienced beatings, imprisonment, and desertion by friends, which could have plunged him into the depths of depression, he was able to say, "Who shall separate us from the love of Christ? Shall trouble or hardship or persecution or famine or nakedness or danger or sword? . . . For I am convinced that neither death nor life, neither angels nor demons, neither the present nor the future, nor any powers, neither height nor depth, nor anything else in all creation, will be able to separate us from the love of God that is in Christ Jesus our Lord" (Romans 8:35,38-39).

Isn't that incredible? You are a brand new creation, a child of God, totally forgiven, righteous in God's sight, perfect and complete, a part of the body of Christ, free, and totally loved by the Father. This is who you are—the real you—not because of what you do or don't do, but because of the love and grace of God that has been lavished upon us through Jesus Christ.

But, you say, can I experience all of this on a daily basis?

## How to Experience the Real You

As Christians, we live by faith. What is faith? It's "being sure of what we hope for and certain of what we do not see" (Hebrews 11:1). We cannot physically see that we are children of God, totally forgiven, clothed in Christ's righteousness, and perfect in God's sight. These are spiritual truths that can be experienced only by faith. And the object of our faith must be Christ and His Word.

Faith is like swallowing. You could say to me, "Bob, you've got to swallow to live," and I'd agree. However, I can also swallow and die, can't I? It's not *swallowing* that enables you to live; swallowing *food* enables you to live. You can also swallow poison and die, using the identical mechanism. So it is with faith. It is *Christ* who enables me to live spiritually. He is to be the object of our faith.

Beth is a fine example of someone whose life was changed by these truths. Beth grew up in a Christian home, accepted Jesus at age eight, and married a Christian man. She struggled with some of the misconceptions many Christians face.

"I reached a point in my life where I questioned whether or not I was a Christian," she said, "because I didn't have the joy that was supposed to come with my salvation. I knew I had accepted Jesus Christ into my heart, but I thought maybe I wasn't sincere enough. I felt He expected more from me than I could offer or was willing to give. Guilt and fear became frequent emotions until I understood that Jesus didn't expect anything from me except to walk by faith in Him."

All of us want to know what we are supposed to do as Christians. We want to know what God's will is for us. The disciples were no different. They came to Jesus and asked Him, "What must we do to do the works God requires?" (John 6:28).

Jesus answered, "The work of God is this: to believe in the one He has sent" (John 6:29). What God requires is for us to trust and believe Him. Faith concentrates on Jesus Christ, not on ourselves. Beth came to this understanding at one of our conferences. Her husband, Bob, observed the changes that resulted.

"Prior to that, Beth's friends would sense her depression and self-focus," said Bob. "After the conference they noticed a drastic change in her. She was far more at ease and desirous to get involved with people. They commented to Beth about the changes that were evident in her life. It's amazing how much we change simply by knowing and resting in who we are in Christ."

Just for a moment, let's think about the implications of the object of our faith. Either Christ did everything for us, or He didn't do anything. God's grace must be total or it's not grace. Either all of your sins are totally forgiven, or none of them are forgiven. Eternal life must last forever, or it is not eternal life. Salvation must be total or it's not salvation. You either stand clothed in the righteousness of Christ, or you have no righteousness at all.

The object of our faith is Christ and His finished work. The apostle Paul said, "If anyone is in Christ, he is a new creation; the old has gone, the new has come!" (2 Corinthians 5:17). He also said, "I have been crucified with Christ and I no longer live, but Christ lives in me. The life I live in the body, I live by faith in the Son of God, who loved me and gave Himself for me" (Galatians 2:20).

In other words, we are transformed. Let's return to our butterfly illustration. You don't look at a butterfly and say, "Look at that good-looking converted worm." It's not a worm anymore; it's a butterfly. How did it get to be one? Well, it was a worm that was converted. But now it is a brand new creation. So it is with us when we become Christians. We are brand new creatures in Christ. Have you ever referred to yourself as an old sinner saved by grace? God doesn't look at you that way. Rather, He calls you a saint. How did you get to be a saint? You were an old sinner who was saved by grace. You are now a new creature made in His image for His good works.

How do I experience my new identity in Christ? In Romans 6:11 (KJV), Paul uses the word "reckon." It means "consider," or "live knowing that the following is true." We reckon ourselves dead to sin—dead to our old identity in Adam. But we reckon ourselves alive to Christ—to our new identity as children of God. So let go of the past attitudes you had about yourself and hold onto the truth of what God says about you. You are dead to sin; you are alive in Christ. That's the truth! That's what God says about you. It's a fact: It will last forever. The opinions of man can and do change. But God's truth about your identity will never change.

## Letting Go of the Past

Paul says in Philippians 3:13, "Brothers, I do not consider myself yet to have taken hold of it (the goal of Christ for us). But one thing I do; Forgetting what is behind and straining toward what is ahead, I press on toward the goal to win the prize for which God has called me heavenward in Christ Jesus."

For Paul to press on meant letting go of the past. This reminds me of a cute story about how monkeys are caught. In the South Pacific Islands, the natives take a coconut, cut a hole in it, and place some sweet beans inside. The monkey comes along and finds the coconut, puts his hand in the hole, and grabs the beans. But when he grabs hold of the sweet beans, his fist becomes too big and is unable to come back through the hole. Amazingly, he will not let go of the beans. In the morning, the natives come by and pick up the monkey still clutching his beans.

Friends, we must let go of the past! If you're holding onto some beans—past circumstances, negative opinions about yourself, or whatever—will you let go of them now? Of course we have made mistakes in our past. Who hasn't? That's why the Lord Jesus Christ looked down in mercy and love and forgiveness and said, "I'm going to provide a way whereby people can be reconciled to Me because I love them." He died and rose again for us not because we're good people, but because we needed help.

There's no need for us to have a pity party. We don't need to beat ourselves to death over the past. We are free in Christ. That freedom is available to all who let go of their past opinions about themselves and stand firm in the truth of who they are in Christ.

So, let go of those past attitudes, grab on to who God says you are, and enter into His presence with thanksgiving and praise!

# 10

## *Controlled by the Love of God*

The phone call came to our office quite unexpectedly. In fact, I thought it was ironic that it came at a time when I was in the process of writing this chapter.

I had known Susan for over a decade but had not seen her for a few years. I remember when she and her husband first attended our fellowship. She was excited about Christ, His love, and learning about God's Word. My heart sank as I listened to the panic and fear in her voice.

"I've done something terribly wrong," said Susan. "Legally, I can go to jail for what I've done. Bob, does God still love me?"

Susan was humiliated by what she had gotten herself into at work. The circumstances surrounding her getting caught was driving her to question God's love for her. It was clear to me that what she was so excited about when she first came to Christ—*His love*—was the very thing that she now was questioning. Susan may have intellectually known about God's love and even talked about it, but she was never convinced in her heart of this central truth. Thus, Susan's beliefs were shaky from the start, but this wasn't evident until this circumstance came about. Now that a terrible storm was blowing her way, she had forgotten and even doubted God's love, compassion, mercy, power, and willingness to help her in her time of need.

In contrast, I know of a young married couple who responded to a traumatic situation in a way that could only be described as supernatural.

The husband and wife were robbed and abducted at gunpoint and, while the woman was being raped, her husband was forced to watch the horrible scene. They said that after they were abducted from their garage and forced into the trunk of their car with their hands bound, they prayed and repeated a verse from John 16:33 in hopes of surviving the ordeal: "These things I have spoken unto you, that in me you might have peace. In the world ye shall have tribulation: but be of good cheer. I have overcome the world" (KJV). They did not question God's love, nor did they wonder if they were being punished for some reason. They put their lives in God's hands and experienced His peace.

Several months later, at the trial, the same peace was evident in their lives. They commented to reporters, "We feel no hatred toward the three men, and we will let God put our lives back together and guide our steps. We can both honestly say that we haven't felt anger, bitterness, or hatred toward any of them," said the husband. "By God's grace, we haven't experienced any of that."

The difference between Susan's situation and the married couple's experience is that Susan was never really convinced about God's love for her. In contrast, the married couple already knew beyond a shadow of a doubt and were convinced about God's love for them, and when the traumatic event happened, they had a solid foundation upon which to stand.

We need to stand on a solid foundation if we are going to weather the storms of life, and we are guaranteed of sure footing if we have been *convinced* about the things of God. However, becoming convinced of God's love is something we cannot force ourselves to do. It takes trials and tribulations, and the ministry and power of the Holy Spirit in the midst of these to show us where we are in our relationship with Him and enable us to see life from His perspective.

But who exactly is the Holy Spirit? What is His purpose in our lives? And can He truly give us the power to live above our circumstances? Let's take a few moments to find some answers to these important questions.

## The Person of the Holy Spirit

*The Holy Spirit is God, co-equal with God the Father and God the Son.*

Many people have difficulty understanding the doctrine of the Trinity. For centuries, people have wrestled with this truth, trying to understand it. I once heard someone quote a college professor who said, "Anyone who denies the Trinity will lose his soul, but anyone who tries to understand the Trinity will lose his mind." I think I agree with him.

As finite human beings, we cannot fully comprehend the implications of the Trinity. All we know for certain is that the Scriptures say that God is one God. Yet just as clearly, the Scriptures declare that there is God the Father, God the Son, and God the Holy Spirit. The only intelligent conclusion I can reach is that God does not consist of three separate entities—He is not $1 + 1 + 1 = 3$—but that somehow there are three distinct persons wrapped up within the same God—perhaps $1 \times 1 \times 1 = 1$.

Maybe you don't understand that. I'm not sure I do, either. People have tried to explain the Trinity with examples from nature. They say that a person consists of body, mind, and soul. The compound $H_2O$ can exist in three forms—solid, liquid, and vapor. Depending on the temperature, you can have water, ice, or steam. An egg consists of a yolk, the white, and the shell. Which part is the egg? All three of them together equal an egg. But I don't know if any of these examples can help us to understand the Trinity. In actuality, they just help us to understand nature.

The evidence for the Trinity appears throughout the Bible. The most common Hebrew word used for God in the Old Testament is *Elohim*. Though used in the singular, it literally means "plural of majesty." In the creation account, God said, "Let *us* make man in *our* image" (Genesis 1:26). Who are the "us" and "our"? In the next verse, we read that God created man in *His* own image. Later, in Genesis 11:7, God says, "Come, let *us* go down and confuse their language." What does "us" refer to? The fact is that singular and plural references to God are used interchangeably. We cannot fully comprehend it, but the Bible clearly declares it.

In Matthew 28:19, Jesus said, "Go and make disciples of all nations, baptizing them in the *name* [note, singular] of the *Father* and of the *Son* and of the *Holy Spirit*" (emphasis added). The apostle Paul ended the second letter to the Corinthians with these words: "May the grace of the *Lord Jesus Christ*, and the love of *God*, and the fellowship of the *Holy Spirit* be with you all" (emphasis added).

## The Ministry of the Holy Spirit

Why did the Holy Spirit come? I can sum that up in one word: Life! Second Corinthians 3:6 says, "The letter kills, but the Spirit gives life."

Jesus said, "I have come that they may have life, and have it to the full" (John 10:10). But how do we obtain life? Jesus answered that in His talk with Nicodemus. There, He said each man must be "born again": "I tell you the truth, no one can enter the kingdom of God unless he is born of water and the *Spirit*. Flesh gives birth to flesh, but the *Spirit* gives birth to spirit" (John 3:5-6, emphasis added). Without the work of the Holy Spirit, you simply can't experience the life of Christ.

Why do I need life? Every man is born into this world spiritually dead and, therefore, in need of spiritual life. The apostle Paul said in Ephesians 2 that when we were dead in our sins and the uncircumcision of our sinful nature, God made us alive with Christ and forgave all our sins. Jesus said, "I am the resurrection, and the life: He that believeth in me, though he were dead [spiritually], yet shall he live [spiritually]: and whosoever liveth and believeth in Me shall never die" (John 11:25,26 KJV). The reason we need life is because we are dead, and it is the Spirit who does the work of bringing us to life in Christ. Salvation is being raised from death to life.

## The Spirit's Ministry of Conviction

*The Holy Spirit came to prove the world wrong about sin, righteousness, and judgment.* In John 16, when Christ told His disciples He was going away, He said it was good that He was leaving because that was the only way He could then send the Holy Spirit. And the Spirit, He explained, would "convict the world of guilt in regard to sin and righteousness and judgment" (John 16:8).

Why would the Holy Spirit need to do that? Because the world was and is confused about those very matters. The world thinks of sin in reference to actions or doing whatever particular things it thinks are wrong—the filthy five, the dirty dozen, the nasty nine. Everyone has a slightly different list. But what does God say? The Spirit convicts the world of sin "because men do not believe in Me" (John 16:9).

All of the sins of the world were taken away at the cross. Thus the sin of unbelief is the only sin that has to be repented of, which means turning from unbelief to believing in Christ. We, however, tend to grade sins. Adultery is bad—10 points. Stealing is an 8. Lying is maybe a 3. But

God doesn't have any numerical system for sin. It's all the same to Him, and that's why Christ went to the cross—to suffer and die to pay the *total* penalty for *all* our sins. There's only one sin that prevents you and me from spending eternity in heaven, and that is the rejection of Christ and His total provision for us on the cross. The Holy Spirit's role is to convince the world of this truth.

The Spirit also works in people's hearts to convince them they are wrong about righteousness. Why are people wrong about righteousness? Because they think righteousness is something they can earn by their behavior, and thus they can look good in the sight of God. They fall into the trap of comparing themselves to others. "I'm not perfect," they say, "but compared to so-and-so, I'm doing pretty good." They like to think God will grade them on the curve.

But God has only one standard for righteousness, and that's the righteousness of Jesus Christ. Righteousness cannot be received except as a gift from God, and it is received by faith when we first trust Jesus Christ as Savior and Lord. From that point on, we stand in *His* righteousness, not ours (2 Corinthians 5:21).

Finally, the Spirit moves to convince the world it is wrong about judgment. The world is wrong because the ruler of this world, Satan, has already been judged. Satan will not triumph. In fact, he has already been defeated and we are under new ownership.

To illustrate this, let's imagine that you live in an apartment building and your landlord is a mean, vindictive person. Every month, long before the rent is due, he comes and puts pressure on you to be sure you remember to pay the rent. In addition, he has very strict rules and regulations the tenants must abide by or they will be evicted. Because you are one of his tenants, you are under the power and control of this landlord. To say the least, he makes your life miserable.

Then one day you discover that the building you live in has been sold and is now under a new owner. You have a new landlord who, in his personality, is the opposite of the old. He is kind and gentle and tries to make each tenant's stay as enjoyable as possible. However, he allows the old landlord to continue living in the building as a tenant.

Out of habit, each month the old landlord appears and continues to harass you about the rent. For some strange reason, you continue to listen to him. Then one day you suddenly realize you are no longer accountable to him. You are free of his control and are now responsible to a new owner. So from now on, whenever the old landlord comes to your door to put you on a guilt trip, you simply tell him, "Take it up with the new owner."

So it is with our lives. At one time we were under the power of Satan and the world. But now we are under God's ownership and control. Anytime Satan tries to rob us of our joy by putting us under condemnation and guilt, we can merely tell him to take it up with the new owner. Why? Because we are under a new owner. We have died to the old one and are now able to experience a brand new life under the control of the Spirit of God.

## The Spirit's Ministry of Renewing the Mind

The Holy Spirit's convicting work in the areas of sin, righteousness, and judgment is essential for leading people to faith in Christ. After we become believers, the Holy Spirit moves on to another assignment in our lives: He leads us *into all truth about God, yourself, and life* (John 16:13). The apostle Paul calls this "the renewing of our minds."

> I urge you, brothers, in view of God's mercy, to offer your bodies as living sacrifices, holy and pleasing to God—this is your spiritual act of

> worship. Do not conform any longer to the pattern of this world, but be transformed by the renewing of your mind. Then you will be able to test and approve what God's will is—His good, pleasing and perfect will (Romans 12:1-2).

Through the renewal of our mind, we begin to see things, people, and circumstances from God's perspective rather than our own. Normally, we look at life through our own eyes, but God, through the Holy Spirit, elevates our vision to His, and we begin to see things as they really are from His perspective. This—the renewing of our minds—is what enables us to face life's uncertainties with the assurance that God has given us everything that we need for life and godliness, and that faithful is He who called you who will also do it (1 Thessalonians 5:24).

---

*In order to have our minds renewed we must first rely upon the Holy Spirit to reveal the truth about Christ to us.*

---

When a difficult circumstance arises in our lives, the world tells us to do everything within our power to overcome it. Most of us have struggled to do that and have failed. Simply put, the world's solutions may sound good, but they just don't work. In order to have our minds renewed we must first rely upon the Holy Spirit to reveal the truth about Christ to us. Jesus said that the Spirit "will bring glory to Me by taking from what is Mine and making it known to you. All that belongs to the Father is Mine. That is why I said the Spirit will take from what is Mine and make it known to you" (John 16:14-15).

The Holy Spirit teaches us about who Jesus is, His love for us, and His mercy, grace, and forgiveness. He does this so that when we are in the midst of trials and tribulations, we will see that we need what Jesus alone can provide. We need to know and experience the love Jesus demonstrated through His death on the cross (John 3:16; 15:13; Romans 5:8). We need the same mercy He extended to two blind men (Matthew 20:29-34). We need the same compassion that moved Him to feed the 4,000 (Matthew 15:32-38). We need His wisdom. If the Holy Spirit didn't teach us to recognize these truths, then we would never turn to Him in our time of need.

The Holy Spirit also renews our mind by teaching us the truth about ourselves. One of the most amazing passages in the Bible, to me, is Philippians 2:5-8: "Your attitude should be the same as that of Christ Jesus: Who, being in very nature God, did not consider equality with God something to be grasped, but made Himself nothing, taking the very nature of a servant, being made in human likeness. And being found in appearance as a man, He humbled himself and became obedient to death—even death on a cross!"

---

*Christ gave His life for us in order
to live His life through us.
He never intended for us to live
the Christian life in and of ourselves.*

---

Here was Jesus, never anything less than God, walking on this earth as if He were never anything more than a man. What a great contrast to us. Here we are, nothing more than man, strutting around as if we were nothing less than God.

We are quick to elevate ourselves in our pride. Yet we must remember that we are created beings, created to walk in dependence upon our Creator. As the apostle John stated, we can do nothing apart from Jesus Christ (John 15:5).

The Holy Spirit isn't renewing our minds simply to give us information. He is renewing our minds to lead us to a total dependency upon Christ. It is not enough for us to learn what the Word of God says; it's important for us to *experience* and *know* this truth as a reality in our daily lives. The apostle Paul affirmed this when he said, "I urge you, brothers, in view of God's mercy, to offer your bodies as living sacrifices, holy and pleasing to God—this is your spiritual act of worship" (Romans 12:1). Christ gave His life for us in order to live His life through us. He never intended for us to live the Christian life in and of ourselves. Rather, the design is for us to yield our bodies in dependency upon Him. He alone can live the Christian life because He alone *is* the Christian life. It's only as we live in dependency upon Him to control our lives that we will experience His power in our lives.

## The Power of the Holy Spirit

Much of today's teaching on the power of the Holy Spirit has led many Christians to think that God's power is displayed only in dramatic manifestations or miracles. Wild fanaticism by certain groups has caused some Christians to shy away from anything that has to do with the Spirit's power. That is unfortunate, because the Spirit's power can have an important role in our lives.

When we think of the word *power*, we usually think of big, powerful creatures like lions, tigers, and bears. We name our football teams after these powerful beasts—the Chicago Bears, the Detroit Lions, and so on. Who would ever think of naming a football team the Los Angeles Lambs or the Seattle Sheep? Yet the most powerful man who ever lived was called, "The Lamb of God, who takes away the sin of the world!" (John 1:29).

---

*To be controlled by the Spirit
is to be filled with the knowledge of the
breadth, length, height, and depth of
God's love for us in Christ Jesus.*

---

Jesus was the most powerful man who ever lived because He walked in perfect love. He demonstrated the fullness of His love by entering into our death so we could enter into His life. We don't need the power of the Holy Spirit to enable us to do big things for God; rather, we need the Spirit's power so we can understand the love of God as given to us in the person of Christ Jesus.

With that in mind, read carefully these words from the apostle Paul:

> I pray that out of His glorious riches He may strengthen you with power through His Spirit in your inner being, so that Christ may dwell in your hearts through faith. And I pray that you, being rooted and established in love, may have power, together with all the saints, to grasp how wide and long and high and deep is the love of Christ, and to know this love that surpasses knowledge—that you may be filled to the measure of all the fullness of God (Ephesians 3:16-19).

This incredible passage is the key to understanding what it means to be controlled by the Holy Spirit. We do not need the power of God's Spirit to understand the *law* of God. The law is spelled out clearly for all. Rather, we need the Spirit's power to understand the *grace* of God. The law was given to show us our sinfulness and our need for a Savior. Grace is God's unconditional love manifested to us in the midst of our sinfulness. Grace is greater than the law, and cannot be understood apart from the power of the Holy Spirit. To be controlled by the Spirit is to be filled with the knowledge of the breadth, length, height, and depth of God's love for us in Christ Jesus.

## The Teaching of the Holy Spirit

There is no better teacher in the world than the Holy Spirit (John 14:26). When He teaches you, you have been truly taught. Only He can help you to understand the full extent of God's love, because "no eye has seen, no ear has heard, no mind has conceived what God has prepared for those who love Him" (1 Corinthians 2:9).

Without the power of God's Spirit, we would never be able to comprehend the height, depth, width, and breadth of the love of God that is in Christ Jesus. We could still read the Bible and understand what it says, but only the Holy Spirit, who indwells us, can show us what it means. There is a big difference between knowing what something says and knowing what something *means*. Knowing what Scripture says is head knowledge. Knowing what it *means* is heart knowledge.

God wants us to have a heart knowledge of His love, not just a head knowledge. He wants us to be convinced of His love so it will invade our human experience and direct our lives. His is a love that surpasses knowledge.

## Being Filled with the Spirit

The apostle Paul was talking about God's love in Ephesians 5:18 when he said, "Do not get drunk on wine, which leads to debauchery. Instead, be filled with the Spirit." To be filled "with" the Spirit means to be controlled "by" the love and grace of God. We are not to be controlled by wine.

Scripture tells us that God "opposes the proud but gives grace to the humble" (James 4:6). Why? Because the proud say, "I can do it on my own. I don't need God's grace. I can produce my own holiness and righteousness. Why do I need to be clothed in the righteousness of Christ when I can produce my own? Look at all the things I've been doing. No wonder God loves me!"

This kind of attitude prohibits us from ever understanding or receiving God's grace in our daily lives and thus removes from us the opportunity to be controlled by His love. Instead, we are left to live in our own power and, sooner or later, we will come to realize that our power is totally inadequate.

Let's take the tongue, for example. An old Jewish folktale, set in nineteenth-century Eastern Europe, tells of a man who went through a small community slandering the rabbi. One day, suddenly feeling remorseful, he begged the rabbi for forgiveness and offered to undergo any form of penance to make amends. The rabbi told him to take a feather pillow from his home, cut it open, and scatter the feathers to the wind. The man did as he was told and returned to the rabbi. He asked, "Am I now forgiven?"

"Almost," came the response. "You just have to perform one last task: Go and gather all the feathers."

"But that's impossible," the man protested, "for the wind has already scattered them."

"Precisely," the rabbi answered.

Regarding the tongue, the apostle James said, "All kinds of animals, birds, reptiles and creatures of the sea are being tamed [controlled] and have been tamed [controlled] by man, but no man can tame [control] the tongue" (James 3:7). Words are powerful enough to lead to love, but they can also lead to hatred and terrible pain.

If we do not bring our tongues under the control of the Holy Spirit of God, then they will be used to destroy instead of to edify. And keep in mind that the tongue merely expresses what is going on in the heart of man. Until we allow God to renew our minds and bring us to that point of dependency upon Jesus Christ whereby His love can be expressed through us, we will constantly be struggling to perfect in our own flesh that which God said was impossible. It is Jesus who lives in us and promises to complete the work that He began in us.

## God's Love Is the Key

Understanding the need to continually be controlled by the love of God was the key that enabled the apostle Paul to live above his circumstances. As he came to the end of each trial in life, he came out of that experience more assured of God's love than when he entered it. Toward the end of his life, he wrote the triumphant statement that appears in Romans 8:35-39:

> Who shall separate us from the love of Christ? Shall trouble or hardship or persecution or famine or nakedness or danger or sword? As it is written: "For your sake we face death all day long; we are considered as sheep to be slaughtered." No, in all these things we are more than conquerors through Him who loved us. For I am convinced that neither death nor life, neither angels nor demons, neither the present nor the future, nor any powers, neither height nor depth, nor anything else in all creation, will be able to separate us from the love of God that is in Christ Jesus our Lord.

For the apostle Paul, the love of God was more than just words written on a page. He knew from experience the height, depth, length, and breadth of God's love. When the storms of life came, he trusted and relied upon God's love for him.

You will notice that in all his tribulations, Paul concentrated only on the God who can provide us with peace no matter what the circumstance. You'll recall that in chapter 3 we discussed the fact that fear can trigger the onset of depression. It's important, then, that we remember what the Scripture says: "There is no fear in love. But perfect love drives out fear, because fear has to do with punishment. The one who fears is not made perfect in love" (1 John 4:18).

As we come to understand God's perfect love and acceptance, we will discover—miraculously—that our fears are gone...and our depression as well.

# 11

## *An Attitude of Thanksgiving*

All of us have only two options when faced with any kind of adverse circumstance in our lives: One is to respond in fear and anger, which will lead us down the pathway to depression. The other option is thanksgiving which comes from trusting Christ to take our hurts and pains and turn them to work together for our good. But let me emphasize: *Neither response will change your circumstances one iota.* Your response only changes the way you deal with your circumstance.

Second Timothy 3:12 tells us that anyone "who wants to live a godly life in Christ Jesus will be persecuted." Jesus said that a servant is not greater than his master (Luke 6:40), and if people rejected Him, they will reject us. I have come to understand that suffering is a part of the Christian life and should not be perceived as unusual. Still, when rejection comes, it hurts—especially when it comes from those who are close to you.

### Face to Face with Pain

At the beginning of this book I stated that what I was going to write was not theoretical. Both Amy and I recently experienced trying circumstances in which we felt deep emotional pain. During that time, I even considered the temptation to go to sources other than Christ to ease the pain of depression. I camped in the tent of disappointment and allowed myself to go down the spiral of depression. In the midst of the rejection and betrayal, I found myself wanting to know *why* this was happening. I had forgotten that the issue of life isn't *why* but rather *what does God want to teach me.*

God said He would cause all things to work together "for the good of those who love Him, who have been called according to His purpose" (Romans 8:28). While in my difficult circumstance I knew of God's love for me and I knew that I had responded in my love for Him. I knew beyond a shadow of a doubt that I had been called according to His purpose. But there were times when I could not see how He was going to work circumstances together for my good. I knew that God said to "give thanks in all circumstances, for this is God's will for you in Christ Jesus" (1 Thessalonians 5:18), but how could I give thanks for pain? How was I to give thanks for a broken heart over the rejection I received from people I loved?

I knew that I was really in trouble when, during this difficult time, the thought crossed my mind that maybe what I needed to do was to take tranquilizers. But as you may already know, over my years in the ministry, I have been adamant about what I consider to be the deception of the psychological world, which encourages people to alter their minds rather than renew them by taking a pill to gain temporary peace rather than turning to Christ to give lasting peace. When you are in deep pain, however, there is always the temptation to turn to anything to bring temporary relief. Here I was, after teaching for over 20 years the sufficiency of Jesus Christ to meet every need of the human heart, thinking about resorting to the very thing that I had talked against!

Today, I am grateful that the thought of taking tranquilizers crossed my mind because it brought me to my
senses. It was in the depth of my agony that I finally cried
out to God, "I would rather die in this pain than resort to
anything else except You to bring peace to my broken
heart." That's when God flooded my mind with a truth
that I had known but apparently had forgotten: "If God is
for us, who can be against us?" (Romans 8:31). I realized
afresh that the unconditional acceptance we all so desire
in our lives can never be obtained through anyone or anything other than Jesus Christ. We are accepted in the
Beloved. In Him our acceptance is based not on what we
do or don't do but on the fact that God, who is big
enough to maintain the universe and yet small enough to
live in our hearts, has accepted us just as we are and loves
us perfectly.

---

*If God is for us,*
*who can be against us?*

---

Within a few moments, I slept the best I had in months
and woke up with a Scripture on my mind: "Praise be to
the God and Father of our Lord Jesus Christ, the Father of
compassion and the God of all comfort, who comforts us
in all our troubles, so that we can comfort those in any
trouble with the comfort we ourselves have received from
God" (2 Corinthians 1:3-4 KJV). I began to take on a new
attitude in regard to my circumstance. And now I was able
to thank God as He began His process of teaching me understanding and compassion for others who are also in
emotional pain. He encouraged me to continue to teach,
without compromise, with total reliance upon Christ, but

at the same time to be aware of how easy it is to turn to alternative solutions when you are in such pain.

God's Spirit is faithful and is totally committed to teaching and leading us into all truth. Yes, we all can become depressed but we never have to remain in that emotional state. There *is* a way out!

Looking back on the faithfulness of God in the midst of that circumstance, I now realize that His love for me is deeper than I ever dreamed or imagined. I am now totally convinced that nothing can separate me from the love of God (Romans 8:39). In that time I also found out who my true friends were and was overwhelmed by the love of my family. All that's important to me is the fruit that Christ produced in my life. As a result, I know experientially what the apostle Paul meant when he said:

> We have this treasure in jars of clay to show that this all-surpassing power is from God and not from us. We are hard pressed on every side, but not crushed; perplexed, but not in despair; persecuted, but not abandoned; struck down, but not destroyed. . . . All this is for your benefit, so that the grace that is reaching more and more people may cause thanksgiving to overflow to the glory of God. Therefore we do not lose heart. Though outwardly we are wasting away, yet inwardly we are being renewed day by day. For our light and momentary troubles are achieving for us an eternal glory that far outweighs them all. So we fix our eyes not on what is seen, but on what is unseen. For what is seen is temporary, but what is unseen is eternal (2 Corinthians 4:7-9, 15-18).

As one person so beautifully said, "Thus, like the trampled flower whose perfume rises to bless the foot that crushed it, so our hearts can find no bitterness, seek no revenge, wish no ill. The fruitfulness of our own cups must overflow and bless the hand that afflicted us."

## From Tragedy to Triumph

Earlier in this book, I stated that my wife, Amy, knows about adversity. Not only did she go through personal trials and tribulation as a young girl, but she also has had to endure the trials that come from being in the ministry. And yet, she is one of the most stable individuals I have ever met.

Amy grew up in Ukraine at a time in history where men were taken from their families for no apparent reason and either killed or sent to Siberia. Her dad was one of those victims and was snatched from his loving home and sentenced to ten years in a Siberian labor camp.

Amy's family endured many adverse circumstances over the next several years. They were treated as the family of a criminal, and people—including relatives—were afraid to help them. Her mom even had to sell her wedding ring for a piece of bread. The only work she could find was shoveling coal in a nearby community. The pay barely enabled her to keep food on the table.

Amy had no warm clothing or shoes that would allow her to leave the house during the winter months. Her mom had to leave her little three-year-old daughter at home alone while she worked long hours. She would come home from work, dead tired, to a crying and hungry little girl who had been left in the house without heat or toys.

Later, when the German army invaded her village, her family was once again uprooted. They were hauled on a horse-drawn cart to a train depot and loaded into a cattle car that would take them to Nazi Germany, where they would become slave laborers.

After the war, Amy and her family remained in Germany and began to rebuild their lives. In 1956, I was drafted into the Army and stationed in Germany. The first time I saw Amy's innocent, sweet face I knew she was the girl I wanted to marry. I also got to know her mother, who was one of the sweetest women that I've ever known in my life. I can honestly say that in all of the years I knew her, I never heard her say an unkind word about anyone or ever express a spirit of bitterness toward the life she had been forced to live.

During our visits together we spent many evenings talking about Amy's father. Amy's mother would constantly reminisce about their life together with him. He was an orphaned boy who, at an early age, had an accident that left him with a broken leg. It was bent back at the knee in such a way that he had to walk on a crutch. While he was at the orphange, a wealthy couple who greatly admired his intelligence and fine looks expressed interest in adopting him. They arranged for him to go to a hospital so that attempts could be made to straighten his leg. It would take several operations before Fyodor would be able to walk normally.

Unfortunately, during Fyodor's first stay in the hospital, the Russian revolution broke out and his new benefactors had to flee for their lives. Fyodor was once again left alone. Eventually he educated himself and ultimately became an attorney and a professor. He was a very determined, bright young man—a man who was musically inclined and full of life and a desire to make his world a better place. The communist regime found this attitude totally unacceptable and thus sent Fyodor away to Siberia.

Amy's family always talked very fondly about Fyodor and assumed that he died in Siberia. However, after a number of years and through a set of incredible circumstances, (which are fully explained in Amy's book *Goodbye Is Not Forever*), Amy's family learned that her dad had been released from Siberia and was still alive. For the next 20 years, Fyodor tried to get permission to see his family, but to no avail.

Because of the cold war between Russia and the United States, it was totally impossible, from a human standpoint, for him to ever get permission to come to America. We therefore prayed that God would use someone in Russia to share the gospel with Amy's father. Amy herself prayed, "God, I know that it's impossible for me to ever see my dad here on earth. But would you please lead someone to tell him about Jesus so that we can see each other someday in heaven?"

Scripture says that God "is able to do immeasurably more than all we ask or imagine" (Ephesians 3:20), and that proved to be true with Amy and her dad. One Sunday evening as we returned home from church we heard the phone ringing. Amy answered, and the caller was Amy's mom, who asked Amy to please sit down because she had something very important to tell her.

That evening, an airport official had called Amy's brother, who lives in Chicago, asking him, "Are you Thomas Wasylenko?" Thomas answered, "Yes, I am." The airport official said, "There's an old man sitting here in the airport crying. He says he's your dad. Could this possibly be true?"

After 40 years apart, Amy's dad was finally able to see his family again! In Russia, he had been in a hospital, seriously ill. He had written one final letter to the communist officials in Moscow, stating, "I'm an old man lying here in a hosptial dying. My last wish is to kiss my children goodbye. They live in America. I do not want to go there to discuss politics or to sightsee. Please grant me the permission to go."

Miraculously, his request was granted. Fyodor left the hospital and sat in the Moscow airport for three days and three nights waiting for a plane to America. He arrived with only the clothes that he had on his back. After a few days of recuperating and visiting with his son Thomas in Chicago, Amy's dad, along with her sister Ann, flew to

Dallas to see our family. I'll never forget the sight of this little man coming off the airplane, holding onto his cane. The minute we saw him, we loved him.

Fyodor thought he had come to America merely to visit, but God had an even greater plan for his life.

Amy began talking to him about the Lord Jesus Christ and the love of God. At times her father would say, with a bewildered look in his eyes, "Little daughter, where did you hear these words? These are words of love I have never heard before." She explained that they were from Jesus, and Fyodor said he wanted to know more about this man called Jesus. On the second day of his visit, we were sitting at the breakfast table. Amy and I handed him a Russian-language Bible and asked him to read through the third chapter of John.

As he read through John 3:16, I asked Amy to tell him to put his first name in that passage. Amy's dad looked up at me, and then back at the Scripture, and began reading, "For God so loved Fyodor that He gave His one and only Son, that whoever believes in Him shall not perish but have eternal life." Immediately, tears welled up in his eyes as he put his head on the table and accepted the living Christ into His heart as his personal Lord and Savior. I've never seen such an instant transformation in a man.

I grew to love Fyodor deeply, and we spent many hours talking about his past. One evening he shared about the night when he was taken away from his family. He had kissed his son and older daughter; then, without a word, he kissed his wife. He then bent over, gently took Amy's little hand and kissed it, and whispered, "Goodbye. I'll see you soon, my little daughter." Caught up in his thoughts, he tearfully commented, "I would have crawled on my hands and knees from Russia to America in order to see my family before I die."

Within a few days, Amy, her sister Ann, and Fyodor flew to Ann's home in Pennsylvania, where he was to see Amy's mom for the first time after 40 years of separation.

That weekend, they all assembled in the backyard for the first and only Wasylenko family portrait. Amy's mom and dad stood next to each other. Gently her dad slipped his arm around her mom's waist. It was a bittersweet moment. How eloquently that gesture expressed the tragedy of two people torn apart by the ravages of war and forced, through uncontrollable circumstances, to travel in opposite directions. Now they stood next to each other with the family they had brought into this world.

Amy placed her arm around her father and said, "I love you, dad." He looked at her tenderly and responded, "I not only love you, I adore you! Like an angel, you opened my eyes to who Jesus is." He then held up his cane toward heaven and triumphantly shouted, "Slava Bogu!" which means, "Praise God!"

After the family visit, Amy's father had to return to Russia. During his remaining years there, he wrote several short notes expressing his feelings for his family. I would like to share with you just a few of these:

> After living through everything possible, horrendous and frightening, how indescribably happy I am now that I have seen you, my precious children. Little Amy, wiping away tears from my eyes, you have removed the dark scales from them and opened them to light and I have experienced God. Ann, you have scrubbed and washed the dirt off of my body and embraced me warmly like a loving mother. I recovered, felt better, and I was refreshed. I recovered completely. Your father.

In another, he wrote:

> Truly, Amy, I wanted to see you. For you grew up, matured, and had children without my presence. You didn't know me and I didn't know you. You, my little daughter, loaded such joy into my inner being, my soul, that I feel like I've been born again in this world. My days have turned lighter and brighter and the nights have turned warmer. You took the film off of my eyes, now I can see. May God give us friendship and unity, peace and quietness, pure love, truth, and goodwill among people. Your father.

His last and final letter stated:

> I'm glad that after 40 years I got to see you, my dearest little daughter. To me you are the closest, the dearest, and most precious. Intuitively, I feel your warm sincerity toward me. Your father.

## We're Important to God

You see, my friend, God has a plan that is bigger than all of us. When you look back on the circumstances Amy's family endured, you can see that God's hand was on them all the time. Amy's father was a little orphaned boy who, restricted by a stiff leg, lived most of his life under persecution and imprisonment. To the world, he was totally insignificant, but to God he was so precious that He plucked him out of Russia and brought him to America in order to draw him to Himself. All of the family had lived through years of great danger and suffering, but ultimately, nothing could harm them until God fulfilled all that He had planned for them. Today, Amy's mom and dad are with the Lord, and someday all of us will meet again. Indeed, God *does* cause all things to work together for good to those who love Him!

When you experience adversity, there truly is an alternative to anger and self-pity, and that is to walk by faith in the One who loves you and gave Himself for you. As His child, you are the recipient of His love and care and are a part of a plan that is so much bigger than yourself. *That's* why you can give thanks in all things.

---

## *God has a plan that is bigger than all of us.*

---

### Having a Thankful Spirit

Faith always says thank you. Faith thanks God for who He is, for who you are, and for what you are becoming in Him. Faith enables you to give thanks in everything because you truly do believe God's promise that He will work everything together for good in the lives of His children. Giving thanks also enables you to live in the present instead of worrying about the past or the future. Jesus said, "Who of you by worrying can add a single hour to his life? Since you cannot do this very little thing, why do you worry about the rest?" (Luke 12:25-26).

Thanksgiving is an essential part of renewing your mind; it enables you to begin to see things from God's perspective rather than your own. It's the dynamic for resting in God's peace and, perhaps, even more important, is the visible evidence to yourself that you're walking by faith and dependency upon Christ.

One of the most moving stories I know about someone having a thankful spirit came from a little girl named Mary. At a youth camp in Northern Califronia, a group of young people spent the week learning about Christ. At the end of their time together they had a campfire meeting, and each person was encouraged to express a statement of thanksgiving. Most of the young people said what you would expect to hear in the midst of their beautiful surroundings: "I thank God for this beautiful scenery, and for the moon and stars." Some said, "I thank God for the joy I see in the faces of my brothers and sisters in Christ." All of them talked about things they could see, until it was Mary's turn to share.

For a moment, Mary said nothing. Then she gave a confident smile and said, "I thank God that I was born blind!"

Stunned, one of the girls lovingly asked, "Mary, how could you feel that way?"

Mary's answer was one that clearly indicated the depth of her understanding of the grace of God. She said, "Because this week I've learned about the love of God. I now realize that God, in His sovereignty, chose to give me virgin eyes, and the very first thing that I will ever see is my Jesus."

Now *that* is a victorious life! That is the kind of thankful spirit God is desirous of producing in you and me. That is what allows us to live above our circumstances instead of under them. That is true contentment—thanking God for whatever circumstance you find yourself in. This is where victory lies—in Him. It is walking in the Spirit, which means walking by faith in the unconditional love and grace of God.

A few years ago, I ran into an old friend of mine whom I had not seen for a long time. I asked him the familiar question, "How are you doing?" His reply was, "I guess I'm doing okay under the circumstances." My reply to him was, "What are you doing under there?"

God never called us to live *under* our circumstances, but *above* them. We are told in the Scriptures that God has "made us sit together in heavenly places in Christ Jesus" (Ephesians 2:6 KJV); therefore, we have the distinct privilege of looking *down* on our circumstances and seeing them from God's perspective rather than man's. It is only as we learn the secret of observing life through the eyes of our Lord Jesus Christ that we will continually experience the freedom God has called us to—a freedom that's real and everlasting!

# A Personal Invitation

If after reading *Living Above Your Circumstances* you realize that you have never accepted God's offer of salvation in Jesus Christ—or if you simply are *not sure* whether or not you are in Christ—I invite you to receive Him right now. John 1:12 says, "to all who received Him, to those who believed in His name, He gave the right to become children of God." In Christ is total forgiveness of sins, total acceptance, and eternal life.

Salvation is a free gift that you accept by faith. You are not saved by prayer, but prayer can be a way of concretely expressing your faith in Christ. For example, here is a suggested prayer:

> *Lord Jesus, I need You. Thank You for dying for the forgiveness of my sins and for offering me Your righteousness and resurrected life. I now accept by faith Your gift of salvation. Through Your Holy Spirit, teach me about Your love and grace and about the new life that You have given me. Begin the work of making me into the person You want me to be. Amen.*

Again, there is nothing magical about praying these words. God is looking at the heart that trusts fully in Him.

If you have received Jesus Christ through reading *Living Above Your Circumstances,* if your life has been impacted in other ways through the ministry of this book, or you would like more information about our ministry, I would very much appreciate hearing from you. May God bless you with a deep personal understanding and experience of His matchless love and grace!

My mailing address is:

Bob George
People to People
2300 Valley View Lane, Suite 200
Dallas, TX 75234

## *Other Books by*
## *BOB GEORGE*

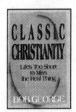 

### Classic Christianity
### Classic Christianity Study Guide

### Growing in Grace
### Growing in Grace Study Guide

Classic Christianity Audio Book

Classic Christianity Illustrated

Classic Christianity Study Series
- A Closer Look at Faith, Hope, & Love
- A Closer Look at the Finality of the Cross
- A Closer Look at Jesus Christ
- A CLoser Look at Law and Grace
- A Closer Look at the Reality of the Resurrection
- A Closer Look at the Truth About Prayer
- A Closer Look at the Word of God
- A Closer Look at Your Identity in Christ

Complete in Christ

# Additional Materials

### Experiencing Victory Over Depression
(Video and audiotape series)
The spiral into depression begins in our minds—our thoughts. Learn how to avoid the trap of self-pity and despair and experience the reality of Christ as your hope in the midst of *any* hopeless situation.

### The New Covenant: Walking in the Fullness of God's Grace
(Videotapes)

Do you experience fear, guilt and frustration in life? Certainly, this is *not* what walking in the fullness of God's grace means. In this series, you will learn how to let go of trying to earn God's acceptance and rest in what He has provided you through Jesus Christ.

### How to Have a Proper Self-Image
(Four audiotapes)

If you do not have a proper self-image before the storms of life hit, you can drown in a sea of uncertainty. Discover the difference between a *good* self-image and a *proper* self-image, and understand fully who you are in Christ.

### The Battle for Control
(Two audiotapes)

During the trials of life we are constantly torn between casting our cares on Jesus and trying to control circumstances ourselves. This battle is waged in every believer. In this insightful series, Bob George explains how you can overcome in this battle and live above your circumstances.

*For more information, please write to:*
**Bob George**
c/o People to People Ministries, 2300 Valley View Lane, Suite 200
Dallas, TX 75234, or call 1-800-727-2828